FOREWORD

Dominica has been described as a 'giant plant laboratory'. It is a treasure island of undisturbed nature, hardly changed for thousands of years where cultural and historical legacies handed down are still alive and active, and have contributed to our diversified product. This diversity extends to our marine environment which offers the best in diving, snorkeling and other aquatic activities. We are proud of the fact that our people have preserved their natural friendliness.

A strong conservation policy has allowed for the survival of our plant and animal life and has ensured the protection of our natural resources and earned us the name 'Nature Island of the Caribbean'.

We are very pleased to be associated with Moorland Publishing in the creation of a guide to Dominica. This guide has captured our natural attractions and provides comprehensive information on Dominica. This guide will serve to expose our island to persons who will want to share and experience our adventure and hospitality. We look forward to welcoming you.

Marie-José Edwards (Ms)
Director of Tourism

Carib Point

Vielle Case

Toucari Bay
Douglas Point
Douglas Bay

Anse Soldat
Chudal Blanc Point
Anse de Mai

Point Baptiste
Grand Baptiste Bay

L' Anse Noir

Woodford Bay

N
W — S

Cabrits
National Park

Portsmouth

Fort
Shirley

Purple Turtle Beach

Cabrits Cruise
Ship Berth

Prince
Rupert Bay

Indian River

Hampstead
Calibishie

Crompton Point

Glanvillia

Wesley

Londonderry Bay

Marigot

Melville
Hall Airfield

Pagua Bay

Dublanc
Bioche

Colihaut

Morne Diablotins
Northern
Forest Reserve

Salybia

Caribe
Territory

L' Escalier Tête Chien

Sineku

Coulibistri

Central Forest
Reserve

Castle
Bruce

Salisbury

Méro

Macoucherie
Rum Factory

Emerald
Pool

Grand
Marig
Bay

Saint Joseph

Layou

Petite
Soufrière

Saint
Sauveur

Rosalie

Rodney's Rock

Morne Trois Pitons

Dominica
Coconut
Products

Boeri Lake

Belfast

Mahaut

Freshwater
Lake

Massacre

Middleham Falls

Cochrane

Morne Trois Pitons
National Park

Bout
Sable
Bay

Canefield Airport

Old Mill Cultural Centre

Papillote Wilderness Retreat
and Nature Sanctuary

Boiling Lake

La
Plain

Trafalgar Falls

ROSEAU

Wotten
Waven

Wotten Waven
Sulphur Springs

Valley of
Desolation

Boetica

Victoria
Falls

Loubiere

Giraudel

Morne
Anglais

Delices

Pte Michel

Bellevue
Chopin

Petite Savane

Stowe

Fond Saint Jean
Geneva

Berekua
Grand Bay

Dominica

Pte Guignard

Soufrière

Soufrière Bay

Scotts Head

Scotts Head Village

Soufrière
Sulphur
Springs

Fort Cachacrou

Martinique Channel

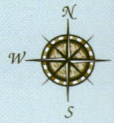

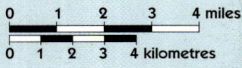

0 1 2 3 4 miles
0 1 2 3 4 kilometres

CARIBBEAN SUNSEEKERS
Dominica

Don Philpott

MPC

Published by:
Moorland Publishing Co Ltd,
Moor Farm Road West, Ashbourne,
Derbyshire DE6 1HD England

ISBN 0 86190 592 X

British Library Cataloguing in Publication Data:
a catalogue record for this book is available from the British Library.

Colour origination by: Reed Reprographics, Ipswich, England
Printed in Hong Kong by Wing King Tong Co Ltd

ACKNOWLEDGEMENTS:
Charles A. Savarin, Marie-José Edwards and Athenia Henry of the Dominica National
Development Corporation Department of Tourism, Fort Young Hotel, Layou River Hotel,
American Airways LIAT and Ron Mellow

PICTURE CREDITS:
Front cover: Anse de Mai near Hampstead on the north coast (main photo), Layou River Resort
(inset). Back cover: packing bananas for export near Rosalie. Title page: Near Calibishie.
All photographs are from the MPC Picture Collection.

MPC Production Team:
Editor: Tonya Monk
Editorial Assistant: Christine Haines
Designer: Dick Richardson
Cartographer: Mick Usher

DISCLAIMER

While every care has been taken to ensure that the information in this book is as
accurate as possible at the time of publication, the publishers and author accept
no responsibility for any loss, injury or inconvenience sustained by anyone using
this book.

Your trip to the Caribbean should be a happy one, but certain activities such
as water sports should be approached with care and under proper supervision
when appropriate. It is also in your own interests to check locally about flora and
fauna that it is best to avoid.

Contents

KEY TO SYMBOLS USED IN TEXT MARGIN AND ON MAPS

🚶 Recommended walks

♣ Parkland

🏰 Castle/Fortification

✳ Other place of interest

⚓ Beach

⛵ Water sports

⛪ Church/Ecclesiastical site

🏛 Museum/Art Gallery

🏞 Beautiful view/Scenery, Natural phenomenon

🐦 Birdlife

✈ Airport

🌸 Garden

KEY TO MAPS

——— Main Routes (Surfaced)   〰 Rivers

HOW TO USE THIS GUIDE

Enjoying as much sun and fun on a vacation is everyone's dream. *Caribbean Sunseekers: Dominica* will help to make this dream come true.

Your guide has been designed in three easy to use sections. 'Before You Go' is packed with detailed information on the island, its history, geography, people, culture, food and much more. 'Touring and Exploring Dominica' is a comprehensive itinerary covering the island with a series of useful and practical motoring or walking tours. Many places are off the beaten track and not on the usual tourist circuit. 'Traveller's Tips' arranged in alphabetical order for easy reference, lists practical information and useful advice to help you plan your vacation before you go and while you are there.

Distinctive margin symbols in the text and on maps, plus places to visit highlighted in bold enable the reader to find the most interesting places with ease.

Before You Go

THE NATURE ISLAND OF THE CARIBBEAN

The Commonwealth of Dominica is the most unspoilt of the Windward Islands and its natural, often wild beauty, is one of its greatest charms. It should not be confused with the the Spanish-speaking Dominican Republic 500 miles (800km) to the west in the Greater Antilles.

Dominica (pronounced Dom-ee-nee-ca) boasts some of the finest unspoilt beaches and reefs in the Caribbean and has a spectacular, rugged mountain interior. There is excellent hiking, great diving, wonderful watersports, yachting and windsurfing. The food is spicy and exciting and the rum is as warm as the island's genuine welcome and the sun which seems always to shine.

Traditional boat building on the east coast

GETTING TO DOMINICA

By Air — Dominica's airports do not allow large jets, and access by air is usually via connecting flights from the main gateways of Antigua, Barbados, Guadeloupe, Martinique, Puerto Rico, St. Maartens and St. Lucia. There is a Dominica Information Desk in the arrival terminal of V.C. Bird International Airport in Antigua which is open daily to assist travellers to Dominica.

International airlines serving these gateways include American Airlines, Air Canada, Air France, Air Martinique, BWIA, British Airways, Continental and Lufthansa. Regional and connecting services are provided by Air Guadeloupe, Cardinal Airlines, LIAT, WINAIR and Caribbean Air Services.

LIAT, Air Guadeloupe, Air Martinique and Cardinal Airlines operate most of the connecting flights between Dominica and the gateways.

LIAT flies between Dominica and Anguilla, Antigua, Barbados, Barbuda, Caracas, Grenada, Guadeloupe, Martinique, Montserrat, Nevis, Port of Spain, San Juan, St. Croix, St. Kitts, St. Lucia, St. Maarten, St. Thomas, St. Vincent and Tortola.

Carib Express which was launched in 1995 is based in Barbados, and operates the only jet service between the islands, flying 146s which require relatively short runways for take-off and landing. It flies between Barbados, Grenada, Dominica (Melville Hall), St. Lucia (Vigie), St. Vincent, as well as Tobago and Port of Spain.

The main airport is at Melville Hall on the north-eastern coast, about 36 miles (60km), or 1 hour drive from the capital Roseau. There is a second and smaller airport at Canefield which opened in 1982, and which is about 4 miles (6km) north of Roseau.

On airline tickets Melville Hall is denoted by the letters DOM, and Canefield by DCF. As you may fly into one airport and depart from the other, check your ticket to make sure you know which one you should be at, as you are unlikely to have enough time to get from one to the other if you make a mistake.

Cardinal Airlines are the only Dominican run airline and run a non-stop daily service on two Beech C99 15-seaters to St. Maarten, Antigua, Barbados and Guadelope. The aircraft are also available for charter.

By Sea — There are entry facilities for yachts at Portsmouth, the main port, and Roseau, which also has a deep water facility at

Woodbridge Bay, just to the north of the town. The facility can take vessels with a draft of up to 30ft (9m) and up to 500ft (152m) long. The port has modern container facilities. There are regular sailings between Dominica and major international ports in North America, Europe and the Caribbean.

There are scheduled ferry services between Dominica and Martinique and Guadeloupe operated by Caribbean Express and Madikera. Seats should be reserved during the high season.

Cruise ships regularly visit Dominica visiting either Roseau or Portsmouth.

HISTORY

The first settlers were the ancestors of the peaceful Arawak Amerindians, who migrated from South America to Dominica via the other Windward Islands. The first of these primitive settlers arrived 5,000 years ago, and about 2,000 years ago, the first Arawaks arrived. They were wonderful artists and craftsmen, and produced elaborate, decorative pottery to prove it.

They lived in small coastal communities, wore few clothes but decorated themselves with tattoos, feathers and beads, and were skilled potters.

They were ousted by the warlike Caribs who migrated north along the same route around AD1000. It is known that the Caribs had a well developed social system and common language throughout the islands. They were led by hereditary kings called 'caciques', while 'shamans' were the religious leaders. Their reputation as warriors was fearsome, and their war canoes could hold more than a hundred men able to paddle fast enough to catch a sailing ship. They were feared by Europeans because of horrific stories about cannibalism with victims being roasted on spits. The Caribs were even said to have a taste preference, thinking Frenchmen were the most tasty, and then the English and Dutch, with the Spanish considered stringy and almost inedible.

Villages were built in inland forest clearings, and each settlement had its own chieftain. Huts were round with timber walls and palm thatched roofs. Early paintings show that they enjoyed dancing, either for pleasure or as part of rituals, and they played ball games. They were primarily fishermen and hunters, although they did

SUNSEEKER HOT SPOTS

BEACHES BETWEEN MARIGOT AND CHUVAL BLANC
some of the most unspoilt beaches in the Caribbean
page 124

BOILING LAKE
volcanic hot pool in the Valley of Desolation
page 85

CABRITS NATIONAL PARK
historic area, natural history, beaches
page 108

CARIB TERRITORY
historic area, traditional arts and crafts
page 121

EMERALD POOL
tropical rain forest setting, wildlife
page 117

INDIAN RIVER
boat trips, wildlife
page 100

LAYOU RIVER
beaches, walks, wildlife, hot pools
page 92

MORNE DIABLOTINS
mountain area offering hikes, wildlife
page 92

ROSEAU
historic town, shopping, restaurants
page 56

SOUFRIÈRE SULPHUR SPRINGS
volcanic area, botanic gardens
page 76

cultivate kitchen gardens, and developed a system of shift cultivation, known as 'conuco'.

The early Spanish recorded their surprise at the Arawak's agricultural techniques, use of fibres and pottery and boat building skills.

When the Caribs achieved dominance, they adopted or adapted many of the Arawak skills especially for farming, and boat building, although their pottery was not as elaborate. Carib homes were rectangular and built using pole frames covered with palm thatch.

The Caribs dominated much of the eastern Caribbean when Dominica was 'discovered' by Christopher Columbus on 3 November 1493. Because he sighted the island on a Sunday, he named it Dominica, which in Latin means God's Day. About 3,000 Caribs, direct descendants of these early settlers' still live on Dominica today and to them the island is still Waitukubuli.

The Caribs discouraged early attempts at settlement because of their hostile behaviour, and many early Europeans sailing in the area avoided the island because of their reputation as cannibals.

There are stories that the Caribs kept Arawaks as slaves penned in corrals and ate them regularly and there are also tales of Europeans captured in battle being eaten. While these tales may have done a lot to enhance the Caribs fearsome reputation, there is little historical evidence to support them.

The first European colonists were French who arrived in 1632, about the same time as French colonies were being established on Martinique to the south and Guadeloupe to the north. The island was then fought over by the French and British until the Treaty of Aix-la-Chapelle in 1748, when the two countries agreed to recognise Dominica as neutral territory. Rather than settling the issue, the treaty provoked even more fighting. French planters continued to settle the island until 1759 when the British captured Dominica. Dominica was formally ceded to Britain in 1763 by the Treaty of Paris, and almost all the French plantations were commandeered and sold by the Crown to English planters. The island fell again to the French, however, in 1778 when an army from Martinique ousted the British.

Preceding page: Box factory supplying cartons for banana growers

Around this time Dominica also became the refuge for large numbers of slaves who had managed to escape from the surrounding islands. These escaped slaves were known as maroons, and the dense forest and mountainous terrain allowed them to remain at liberty.

It was 5 years before the British retook the island and over the next two decades they fought off attacks both from the French and the growing number of maroons who were also encouraging slaves on the island to run away and join them. The maroons raided the settlements and the plantation owners retaliated by raising a tax to recruit a militia, but it was almost useless against an enemy which was able to vanish into the forest.

During the French Revolution, plantation owners loyal to the French Colony fled to Dominica and joined forces with the maroons, promising to free all the slaves if they rose against the British. The French islands had freed all slaves in 1794, but re-introduced slavery in 1802 and it was not until 1848 that they finally introduced Emancipation. British reinforcements were brought in and a running guerilla war was fought with the maroons until 1814 when they were finally

defeated and their leaders publicly executed.

The most serious French assaults were in 1795 when a strong force from Guadeloupe was beaten off, and again in 1805, when French troops landed in force on the island, and burnt the capital Roseau. The French ships had sailed unchallenged into Roseau Bay because they were flying the Union Jack, the British flag. At the last minute they ran down the Union Jack and ran up the Tricolore and then their troops stormed ashore. The French force finally agreed to leave the island only after being paid a ransom of £8,000, which in those days was a fortune.

After Emancipation on Dominica in 1834, the island became a refuge for slaves escaping from the surrounding French controlled islands, and many of these escapees perished crossing the Martinique and Guadeloupe Channels on makeshift rafts and tiny boats. Those that survived the journey were allowed to stay and together with the island's free slaves, moved inland away from the plantations to grow their own crops on small areas cleared in the forest.

Agriculture and fishing were the backbone of the island's

Beaches

Dominica has fabulous beaches, everything you ever dreamed of for a tropical island, miles of sand, a fringe of tall palms for shade, and turquoise clear warm seas. Most beaches consist of very fine volcanic sand which varies in colour from black to grey. There are some golden sand beaches along the north-east coast beyond Melville Hall, and these are often deserted.

Generally the best beaches are on the protected western coast although there are many fine, unspoiled beaches on the northern coast. Beaches on the windier Atlantic Ocean coast tend to have choppier seas but offer excellent surfing and windsurfing, and have fine sandy stretches.

Best beaches are around Portsmouth on the north-east coast, and Calibishie, L'Anse Noir and Woodford Bay on the north coast. The Dominica tourist office states that rivers also offer excellent swimming and are perfectly safe. There are usually pools at the foot of waterfalls in which you can cool off, because most entail a hike in. The colour of sand varies from beach to beach, from the black sand which gives its name to L'Ance Noir, to the white sands of Woodford Bay and Pointe Baptiste which are really millions of tiny fragments of ground coral. The black sand tends to be of volcanic origin and is finer and softer then the sand made from coral and pulverised shells.

There is safe swimming off the golden sands of Woodford Bay, and then a whole host of good beaches to explore. These are Turtle Beach (L'Anse Tortue), L'Anse Noir, Pointe Baptiste, Calibishie, Hampstead, Anse de Mai and Anse Soldat. Access from the main road to many of the beaches is by foot or along old estate roads which are usually passible in good weather with a car. All beaches in Dominica are public but access to them may be via private land so keep to the track. Check locally for any swimming safety risks.

Tanning Safely

The sun is very strong but sea breezes often disguise just how hot it is. If you are not used to the sun, take it carefully for the first two or three days, use a good sun screen with a factor of 15 or higher, and do not sunbathe during the hottest parts of the day. Wear sunglasses and a sun hat. Sunglasses will protect you against the glare, especially strong on the beach, and sun hats will protect your head.

If you spend a lot of time swimming or scuba diving, take extra care, as you will burn even quicker because of the combination of salt water and sun. Calamine lotion and preparations containing aloe are both useful in combating sunburn.

Dominica does not have many beaches and those it has are often empty. This is Purple Turtle Beach near Portsmouth

economy and one of its first industries was the processing of lime juice. A factory was built in 1875 to process juice from limes grown on huge estates around the island. Lime juice was originally produced in quite small quantities for the crews of Royal Navy ships, but became so popular that a new bigger factory was necessary. The Rose's Lime Juice Factory continued to operate until the 1950s and for many decades Dominica was the world's largest producer of lime.

Originally, Dominica was administered as part of the Leeward Islands but was declared a separate colony in 1771. In 1883 it was again administered as part of the Leeward Islands and this continued until 1940, when it became a separate colony as part of the Windward Islands. Dominica joined the West Indies Federation in 1958, and when this was disbanded in 1962, a number of federation options were discussed, leading in 1967 to Dominica becoming a self governing member of the West Indies Associated States in free association with the United Kingdom. It was responsible for all internal affairs.

During the 1970s there were periods of unrest and there were particular problems with the Dreads, so called because they wore their hair in dreadlocks. For a short time they carried out a violent campaign against authority, and took to the mountains before finally being cleared out.

On 3 November 1978, the anniversary of the island's discovery, Dominica achieved full independence with Patrick Roland as the state's first Prime Minister. Alleged complicity in an invasion of Barbados rumoured to have been launched from Dominica, led to his downfall, and Oliver Seraphine became Prime Minister in May, 1979. There was general dissatisfaction at the slow rate of reconstruction following Hurricane David in 1979, and this led to a landslide victory in July, 1980 for the Freedom Party led by Mary Eugenia Charles, a strong advocate of free enterprise, who became Prime Minister. She became the Caribbean's first female Prime Minister. The Freedom Party won again in the 1985 general election, giving Miss Charles her second 5-year term as Prime Minister and she and her party won a third term in elections on 28 May 1990, though with the narrowest of margins. In August, 1993 Brian Alleyne became leader of the Freedom Party although Miss Charles remained as Prime Minister. It had 11 of the 21 seats in the Assembly; The Opposition United Workers' Party had 6, and the United Dominica Labour Party 4. In June 1995 the Freedom Party was defeated in the General Election by the United Workers Party. The new Prime Minister is Edison C. James. His United Workers Party won 11 seats, the Dominica Freedom Party and Dominica Labour Party 5 seats each.

GEOGRAPHY

Dominica lies between the French Guadeloupe to the north and French Martinique to the south in the Windward Islands, themselves part of the Lesser Antilles in the eastern Caribbean.

It is 29 miles (47km) from north to south, 16 miles (26km) wide, and covers 290sq miles (752sq km), making it the largest of the Windward Islands. Roseau in the south-east is the capital and chief port.

The island is of volcanic origin, and in geological terms is relatively new. There are still volcanic vents belching sulphur, and bubbling hot springs. Boiling Lake in the Valley of Desolation is 2,300ft (701m) above sea level and is the second largest lake of its kind in the world. It stands above the vent of a volcano, and

escaping gas creates so much pressure that the water level is often raised by 3ft (1m) or more.

There are dense forest clad mountains in the north and south separated by a central plain formed by the Layou River which flows to the west and Belle Fille River which flows to the east. The Northern Forest Reserve covers 21,770 acres (8,708 hectares), and the Central Forest Reserve 1,013 acres (405 hectares). The highest peaks are Morne Diablotins 4,747ft (1,447m) in the north and Morne Trois Pitons 4,550ft (1,387m) in the southern mountains.

Dense forestation and lack of intensive agriculture has produced a very rich soil, and there are waterfalls and scores of rivers providing clean water. It is said there are 365 rivers, but it is more likely there are around 30 rivers and 335 streams!

Offshore, the waters are warm and brilliantly clear, and considered some of the best diving in the world because of the beautiful coral reefs and and seldom visited wrecks.

Dominica has ten parishes: St. Andrew 69sq miles (179sq km); St. David 40sq miles (104sq km); St. George 21sq miles (54sq km); St. John 23sq miles (60sq km); St. Joseph 46sq miles (119sq km); St.

SHOPPING

Shops are usually open between 8.30am and 1pm and 2pm to 4pm Monday to Friday, and between 8am to around 12noon or1pm on Saturday. Increasingly shops are remaining open at lunchtime.

Best buys are the Carib craft items such as woven straw goods like mats, hats and baskets, pottery, handpainted candles, leather craft, wood carvings and paintings by local artists. There is also wonderful batik, handmade cigars, locally produced coconut oil-based soaps, and a host of spices, spice-based products, preserves and syrups, and of course, island distilled rum.

Shops specialising in local arts and craft include Caribana Handicrafts, Ego, Cotton House Batiks, Tropicrafts, the Woodbridge Bay Craft Market and the NFD Craft Shops at 9 Great Marlborough Street, all in Roseau.

Batik wear and goods are available from Balizier Art and Craft Shop, 35 Great George Street, which also sells paintings by local artists, straw wear and local jewellery. The Bath Estate Pottery sells its hand made products made from local red and white clay.

Dominica Bay Rum is an invigorating body freshener made locally by Shillingford, and widely available in shops, and not to be confused with the rum produced by the island's distilleries. There is D-Special, a good local rum from the Belfast Estate, while the distillery at Macoucherie produces a range of rums. The distillery can be visited Monday to Saturday during working hours which may vary, but the rum is widely available in shops. Macoucherie also produce a rum drink called the Elixir of Bois Bandé, made from the extract of the bark of the Richeria Grandis, locally known as the bois bandé, which for centuries has been used by the Caribs because of its reputed aphrodisiac properties.

Benjashoe flipflops are sold throughout the island and are great for strolling on the beach, and the sandals are fine for walking through the forests or hiking, especially in the wet. Made of plastic, they are lightweight, very cheap, very useful and surprisingly comfortable.

Herbal teas made on the island are very refreshing and invigorating and Blows Agro Products produce a range including peppermint, cinnamon and ginger which are widely available in stores. Bellot Products make a range of locally made juices, jams, jellies and syrups, as well as gourmet coffee and very hot sauces, which are sold in stores and craft shops.

A modern shopping development at Portsmouth

Luke 4sq miles (10sq km); St. Mark 4sq miles (10sq km); St. Patrick 32sq miles (83sq km); St. Paul 26sq miles (67sq km), and St. Peter 11sq miles (29sq km).

The major towns are Roseau, Portsmouth, Marigot, Atkinson, and Mahaut.

THE PEOPLE

The population of around 71,000 is mostly of African descent, with some Europeans and about 3,000 Caribs — the only island with a large and distinctive group of Caribs, direct descendants of the first settlers. Many of the Caribs live in the Carib Territory, a 3,700 acre (1,480 hectare) area on the eastern side of the island with a long stretch of coastline and agricultural interior. The reserve was established in 1903 and is owned by the Carib Indians. They are mainly engaged in farming and fishing, but still practice their traditional skills of weaving and canoe building.

English is the main language, but a French Creole patois is widely spoken, and almost impossible for the visitor to understand. Many place names originate from the original Carib language or from French, and are a reminder of the island's turbulent past. More than three-quarters of

the population are Roman Catholics, but many other denominations are also represented.

Dominica is a presidential republic, with a democratic parliamentary system of Government, and a Chief Executive and House of Assembly. Most of the members of the Assembly are elected, while the remainder, called Senators, are elected or appointed. The Chief Executive is the President who appoints the Prime Minister, who must have the support of the majority members of the House. Members are elected every 5 years and all adults have had the vote since 1951.

CULTURE

The strong Carib culture is evident throughout the island, and particularly so around the north-east coast. It can be seen in the pottery and elaborately woven goods, and particularly in the dug out canoes, which have been made in the same way for centuries. The island's culture has also been influenced by many other nationalities, especially the English and French, and of course, the Africans. It is this merging of different cultures and traditions that has produced the Creole culture that can be seen throughout the Caribbean today. In Dominica a very distinct culture of song, dance and traditional dress has emerged which is a mix of Carib and Creole. The geography of Dominica has also played an important role in helping preserve these old traditions and folk music. Because of the mountains and lack of roads, communities were isolated from each other and developed their own musical styles and dances.

Traditional dances include the bele from West Africa, and the quadrille, which has been adapted from the French, and the jing-ping bands which play at all festive occasions and celebrations, feature the accordion introduced by the French, and the tambal, boomboom and gwaje from Africa.

There has been a revival of traditional African culture and traditions, backed by the Government's Department of Culture, especially of dance, music and costumes, and great efforts have been made to ensure traditional folk songs and dances are preserved.

All these traditions bubble over during Carnival, the island's biggest festival. Carnival is celebrated all over the island, and especially in Roseau where there is a parade of floats and colourful costumes through the town. There are also beauty and costume pageants, and lots and lots of music, from calypso and road marching competition, to jump ups, street parties with music and dancing that last well into the night.

The week long Domfesta, the festival of the arts, is held each July and is a great opportunity to see the amazing range of artistic talent produced by the island.

The other main annual celebration is Independence Day, and this affords another opportunity for the islander's to enjoy all aspects of their culture, particularly music, dance, costume and cuisine. Cultural events are staged throughout Dominica, and late in the evening you can listen to traditional folk songs being played. As many of these are sung in patois, you may not understand the words, but you will still enjoy the music.

ARTS AND CRAFTS

The early Arawaks and Caribs were skilful potters, carvers and weavers and their legacy remains today. Dominica has produced many fine artists and craftsmen, and there are many galleries and stores where you can appreciate their work. In Roseau you can visit the gallery of Kelvin Royer on Virgin Lane, off Bath Road. 'Kelo' is

Above: Packing bananas for export, chiefly to Britain

Facing page: Fort Young Hotel, Roseau, rebuilt after being devastated by Hurricane David

known for his rich local landscapes in oils, and his own abstract style using several colours at once applied with a palette knife.

Earl Etienne also paints wonderful landscapes as well as abstracts, and is also noted for his paintings depicting traditional scenes such as *Bele Dancing*, and *River Washing*. His paintings have been likened to those of Matisse. His work is displayed in the Art Asylum in Massacre, and in Roseau at the H&H Art Gallery and The Garraway.

Arnold Toulon is also a master of colour, and his paintings of landscapes and traditional scenes, have won international acclaim. His works are exhibited at his gallery in Queen Mary Street, Roseau.

Carl Winston is another talented artist but now prefers to carve and sculpt wood rather than paint. He is especially noted for his magnificent relief *Caribs at Indian River*. His works are displayed at Fort Young in Roseau, and the Evergreen Hotel in Castle Comfort. His wife Erma, is an accomplished poet.

Darius David is widely regarded as the 'Father of Art' in Domincia. Self-trained, he has been painting for more than 40 years and prefers to depict historical themes and

traditions, often about places that no longer exist, such as his works featuring the old Hillsborough Bridge and the old Dawbiney Market. His brightly coloured paintings have been exhibited internationally, and have been displayed in Buckingham Palace. His home and studio are at 8 Scotland Lane, off Goodwill Road, and visitors are welcome.

Amos Ferguson started work as a house painter and although he now lives in Nassau, his paintings, which are sold internationally, still feature Dominican scenes and depict the island's life and folklore.

Dominica's writers include Jean Rhys who was born in Roseau in 1890 and brought up on an estate in Grand Bay. She left the island for Europe when aged 16 but several of her books are set in Dominica. Phyllis Shand Allfrey, author of *The Orchid House*, was also born on the island and uses Dominica as the setting for her book.

More traditional handicrafts can be bought at the many craft shops around the island. These include elaborately woven grass mats, and Carib woven baskets and hats. Dominica's straw goods are among the best in the Caribbean and certainly among the cheapest. There is unique Batik art and clothing, pottery and dolls dressed in traditional island costumes, and there is a wide range of products made from plants, fruit and spices grown on Dominica.

Betty Alleyne creates jewellery, both decorative and fun, which is becoming highly collectible. Her pieces, based on island flowers, birds, fish and even fruit, are mostly made from polymer clays and involve intricate working. Her works, sold under the 'Just Us Originals' label are sold at a number of locations around the island, including Papillote Wilderness Retreat at Trafalgar Falls, Ego Boutique and Dive Dominica at Castle Comfort.

The art of batik is highly developed on Dominica. It is a process of dyeing in which patterned areas are covered with wax, which when heated, will not receive colour. The method is used mainly on high quality cottons, and the traditional batik colours are red, green, blue and brown. Multi-coloured effects and intrictate patterns are achieved by repeating the dyeing process several times, with the initial application of wax removed, and another applied

before re-dyeing. Many of the Batik patterns produced on the island feature Dominican landscapes or are strongly influenced by African art.

Batik art and wear, using cotton, silk and rayon, is available from Cotton House Batiks at 8 Kings Lane, and the Artwear Gallery in King George V Street, both in Roseau.

Claudia Henderson, of Cotton House Batiks, uses a special batik method involving hand stitching to produce a marbled effect.

Tropicrafts, at the corner of Queen Mary Street and Turkey Lane, in Roseau, offers a wide range of island handicrafts from woven mats and baskets to rum and curios. It is also a good place to see artisans at work using locally grown grass to produce mats, straw bags, hats, place mats and dolls. The building was formerly a Catholic run industrial school set up to teach women how to use their weaving skills to produce goods which could be sold. Tropicrafts also offers carvings in wood, figures and other items made from cocount shell, local jewellery and handicrafts from the Carib Territory.

Following pages: Hurricane damage, The Botanical Garden, Roseau

The National Development Foundation's Small Business Complex in Great George Street in Roseau, occupies eight small workshops producing and selling local arts and crafts, paintings and herbal teas.

THE ECONOMY

The island is largely dependent on agriculture, fishing and forestry, with tourism of growing economic importance. The island is the least developed of the Windward Islands. Many parts of the island are poor and unemployment is high, but the people are very hard working and, despite their situation, overwhelmingly friendly and hospitable.

Many of the island's main crops, especially bananas, are vulnerable to decisions taken by the European Community in Brussels and international trade agreements such as GATT, and the island is taking steps to diversify and attract new markets.

Bananas, citrus and coconuts are the principle crops, with cocoa, coffee and vegetables also produced and exported. The island's fishing industry was badly hit by Hurricane David in 1979 with most vessels lost, but has now largely recovered. Forestry is

also economically significant and is being developed through careful management of resources. There are deposits of clay and limestone, but the volcanic rock pumice is the most important commercial mineral, used mainly for building.

Most is connected with agriculture such as processing of copra and production of fruit juices, coconut oil, soap and bay oil. There is a furniture industry using local wood, and Portsmouth is the centre of the boat building industry.

Tourism is now developing well thanks to improved roads and communications, and new hotels. Development is strictly controlled, however, to preserve as much as possible, the island's natural state. A number of major resort developments are planned or already under construction, including the 85 room five star eco-resort called Caribbean Shangri la, being built by the Aman group in the Layou Valley. The number of visitors in 1988 topped 36,500 and by 1994 this had grown to more than 65,000 of which 56,522 were tourists, and in the past 6 years the number of cruise ship visitors has increased by more than 1,000 per cent. The tourist board expects the number of visitors to continue to grow because of better marketing, improved facilities and the new cruise liner berth in Roseau.

CLIMATE

The climate is near perfect, especially the 'cooler' months between December and March. Summer temperatures average 90°F (32°C) and humidity is high, while winter temperatures drop to around 85°F (30°C). The 'dry' season is between February and May, and the rainy season between June and October. The difference between the two, according to one islander, is that it does not rain all the time during the dry season. When it does rain, it is usually torrential, but it doesn't generally rain for long, and the sun is soon out again.

Rainfall is heaviest in the mountains, up to 250 inches (635cm) in the rain forests, and lowest around the coast where it averages about 60 inches (150cm) a year. September and October are the most likely months for hurricanes. While the island has fortunately not experienced many hurricanes, Hurricane David which blasted ashore in September,

1979 killed about 250 people and caused massive damage. The island was hit again the following year by the less powerful Hurricane Allen, and in 1989 was swiped by Hurricane Hugo.

FLORA AND FAUNA

The lush vegetation and animal life are part of the island's great charm. The dense forests are full of massive trees, many more than a 100ft (30m) high, and these are draped with vines. Along the branches you can see orchids, ferns and huge air plants. There are palms of all descriptions, giant ferns and bamboos, bananas, coconut groves, hanging breadfruit, mango, nutmeg, cocoa and pawpaw, and the most stunning array of spectacularly coloured flowering plants from giant African tulip trees festooned with scarlet blossom to tiny orchids. Bougainvillea flowers everywhere, there are scores of varieties of hibiscus, frangipani and poinsettia. There are heliconia, also known as the lobster plant, bird of paradise flowers and anthurium everywhere. The flamboyant tree

Following page: This little flower apparently did not grow on Dominica before Hurricane David battered the island

The Manchineel

The manchineel can be found on many beaches and has a number of effective defensive mechanisms which can prove very painful. Trees vary from a few feet to more than 30ft (9m) in height, and have widely spreading, deep forked boughs with small, dark green leaves and yellow stems, and fruit like small, green apples. If you examine the leaves carefully without touching them, you will notice a small pin-head sized raised dot at the junction of leaf and leaf stalk. The apple-like fruit is very poisonous, and sap from the tree causes very painful blisters. It is so toxic, that early Caribs are said to have dipped their arrow heads in it before hunting trips. Sap is released if a leaf or branch is broken, and more so after rain. Avoid contact with the tree, do not sit under it, or on a fallen branch, and do not eat the fruit. If you do get sap on your skin, run into the sea and wash it off as quickly as possible.

is also known as the tourist tree because it bursts into bloom during the summer and is a blaze of colour.

Along the coast you can find swamps, mangroves and marsh woodlands, while inland there are breathtaking walks through tropical rain forests.

Beach morning glory with its array of pink flowers is found on many beaches, and is important because its roots help prevent sand drift. The plant also produces nectar from glands in the base of its leaf stalks which attract ants, and it is thought this evolution has occurred so that the ants will discourage any leaf-nibbling predators. Other beach plants include seagrape and the manchineel, which should be treated with caution.

Of course, the sea teems with brilliantly coloured fish and often, even more spectacularly coloured coral and marine plants. Even if you just float upside down in the water with a face mask on, you will be able to enjoy many of the beautiful underwater scenes, but the best way to see things is by scuba diving, snorkelling or taking a trip in one of the many glass bottomed boats.

There are scores of different multi-coloured corals that make up the reefs offshore. There are hard and soft corals and only one, the fire coral poses a threat to swimmers and divers, because if touched, it causes a stinging skin rash. Among the more spectacular corals are deadman's fingers, staghorn, brain coral and seafans, and there are huge sea anemones and sponges, while tropical fish species include the parrotfish, blue tang surgeonfish, tiny but aggressive damselfish, angelfish and brightly coloured wrasse.

Coastal swamps also provide a rich habitat for wildlife. Tiny tree crabs and burrowing edible land crabs scurry around in the mud trapped in the roots of mangrove trees just above water level. Herons, egrets, pelicans and often frigatebirds roost in the higher branches, the mangrove cuckoo shares the lower branches with belted kingfishers.

The western coastal strip is also the home of Dominica's National Flower, the scarlet Bwa Kwaib, which is indigenous to the island. It is really a deciduous tree which grows to between 10 and 15ft (3 and 4m) high, and it can flower twice a year. It is actually a member of the legume family.

Preceding page: Splitting coconuts before reducing in a furnace

Inland, gardens are generally a blaze of colour with flowers in bloom year round, growing alongside exotic vegetables like yam, sweet potato, and dasheen. Flowering plants include the flamboyant tree with their brilliant red flowers which burst into bloom in early summer, and long dark brown seed pods, up to 2ft (1m) which can be used as rattles when the seeds have dried out inside. Bougainvillea grows everywhere and seems to be in bloom year round in a host of different colours. In fact, the colour does not come from petals but the plants bract-like leaves which surround the small petal-less flowers. There are yellow and purple allamandas, poinsettia, hibiscus, anthurium and multi-coloured flowers of the ixora. The leaves of the travellers palm spread out like a giant open fan, and the tree got its name because the fan was believed to point from south to north, but it rarely does. The flowers attract hummingbirds like the doctorbird, as well as the Carib grackle, a strutting, starling-like bird with a paddle-shaped tail, and friendly bananaquit. You can also spot tree lizards, and the larger geckos which hunt at night.

Along roadsides and hedgerows in the countryside,

you can see the vinelike caralita, calabash with its gourd-like fruits, tamarind and distinctive star-shaped leaves of the castor bean, whose seeds when crushed yield castor oil.

Areas of scrubland have their own flora or fauna, with plants bursting into colour following the first heavy rains after the dry season. There are century plants, with their prickly, sword like leaves, which grow for up to 20 years before flowering. The yellow flower stalk grows at a tremendous rate for several days and can reach 20ft (6m) high, but having bloomed once the whole plant then dies. Other typical scrubland vegetation includes aloe, acacia, prickly pear and several species of cactus. Fiddlewood provides hard timber for furniture, highly coloured variagated crotons, the white flowered, aromatic frangipani and sea island cotton, which used to provide the very finest cotton. Scrub vegetation also plays host to birds such as the mockingbird, ground dove, kingbird and grassquit, and it is the ideal habitat for lizards.

The rainforests provide the most prolific vegetation with gommier trees, and occasional mahogany trees with their fascinating black and red seeds, much used for necklaces. There are magnificent swathes of giant ferns, towering bamboo groves, enormous air plants, and a host of flowering or variegated plants such as heliconia, philodendron and wild fuchsia. There are some balsa wood trees, the world's lightest wood, the flowering vine marcgravia, and the prolific mountain cabbage palm, and among the foliage and flowers you can find hummingbirds and parrots.

On the steep upper slopes is montane vegetation. Many of the trees have aerial roots and are covered in mosses and lichens, orchids and air plants, and there is usually more ground vegetation because of greater sunlight penetration.

The highest altitudes are covered by elfin woodlands, consisting largely of kaklin trees, palms, mosses, lichens and ferns. The trees are stunted because there is almost always constant wind, little sunlight because of the low clouds, and almost continuous rain.

The animal life on the island is not diverse and there are few large animals. There are frogs and toads which croak loudly all night. The large edible crapaud frog is also known as the 'mountain chicken' because it tastes so good.

There are several species of lizard and geckos, as well as iguana and five species of snake, although none is poisonous and most are quite small. One of the rarest lizards is the tiny and rare 'fantastic' gecko, one of the world's smallest lizards rarely growing to more than 1½ inches (4cm) long. It is usually found close to the beaches, especially around Balali Beach, hiding under leaves.

There are boa constrictors, which the islanders call tête chien, which means dog's head and if you ever see one you will realise why. These normally docile snakes can grow to 8ft (2m) and more, but they are usually killed long before they reach this size. There are lots of legends surrounding this snake with tales of huge serpents attacking men and livestock.

The agouti is common while an unusual animal is the manicou, a member of the opossum family. It lives in trees and forages over huge areas at night, and is not averse to rooting through trash

Facing page: Anthurium lilies, just picked and for sale at the roadside (above), a Flamboyant tree (below)

cans for any delicacies. There are also wild pig in the deepest parts of the forest and its meat is considered a great delicacy.

There are scores of different insects including mosquitoes and midges, but the most impressive are the Hercules Beetle with its massive elongated jaws, and the stick insect, known as 'chouval bwa', which is an expert at camouflage.

There are also fifty-five species of butterflies, many of them huge, and several species of moth.

Lumbering sea turtles also come ashore at night between March and August to lay their eggs in the sand. Both the rivers and seas teem with fish.

There is a hugely rich bird life with more than 160 species, either resident and visitors on migration. There are two species of parrot which are only found on Dominica — the Imperial Parrot or Sisserou, Dominica's national bird, which has a mauve breast and green wings, and the smaller red-necked parrot, also known as the Jaco. Both are endangered species. A Government conservation scheme includes a breeding programme of captive birds, in conjunction with the Jersey Wildlife Preservation Trust. The breeding aviary is in the Botanical Gardens, Roseau, open daily.

There are also bananaquits, mangrove cuckoos, tanagers, ibis, mocking birds, herons, egrets and many others. There are many species of hummingbirds including the tiny blue-headed hummingbird which is also only found on the island and neighbouring Martinique.

Offshore you may sight the magnificent frigatebird, easily recognisable by its size, long black 7ft (2m) wing span, forked tail and apparent effortless ability to glide on the winds. There are brown booby birds, named by sailors from the Spanish word for 'fool' because they were so easy to catch. Pelicans which look so ungainly on land, yet are so acrobatic in the air, are common, as are laughing gulls and royal terns. Several species of sandpiper can usually be seen scurrying around at the water's edge.

If you are really interested in bird watching pack a small pair of binoculars. Mini-binoculars are ideal for island bird watching, because the light is normally so good that you will get a clear image despite the small object lens.

Note: It is an offence to debark any trees, and plants and flowers should not be picked in parks or forest reserves.

As most of the plants, fruits, vegetables and spices will be new to the first time visitor, the following brief descriptions are offered.

Bananas are one of the island's most important exports, earning $176 million in 1994 thus their nickname 'green gold' — and they grow everywhere. There are three types of banana plant. The banana that we normally buy in supermarkets originated in Malaya and were introduced into the Caribbean in the early sixteenth century by the Spanish. The large bananas, or plantains, originally came from southern India, and are largely used in cooking. They are often fried and served as an accompaniment to fish and meat. The third variety is the red banana, which is not grown commercially, but which can be seen around the island. Most banana plantations cover only a few acres and are worked by the owner or tenant, although there are still some very large holdings. A banana produces a crop about every 9 months, and each cluster of flowers grows into a hand of bananas. A bunch can contain up to 20 hands of bananas, with each hand having up to 20 individual fruit.

Although they grow tall, bananas are not trees but herbacious plants which die back each year. Once the plant has produced fruit, a shoot from the ground is cultivated to take its place, and the old plant dies. Bananas need a lot of attention, and island farmers will tell you that there are not enough hours in a day to do everything that needs to be done. The crop needs fertilising regularly, leaves need cutting back, and you will often see the fruit inside blue tinted plastic bags, which protect it from insect and bird attack, sun light and speed up maturation.

Breadfruit was introduced to the Caribbean by Captain Bligh in 1793. He brought 1,200 breadfruit saplings from Tahiti aboard the *Providence*, and these were first planted in Jamaica and St. Vincent, and then quickly spread throughout the islands. It was Bligh's attempts to bring in young breadfruit trees that led to the mutiny on the *Bounty* 4 years earlier. Bligh was given the command of the 215 ton Bounty in 1787 and was ordered to take the breadfruit trees from Tahiti to the West Indies where they were to be used to provide cheap

Following pages: Coconut harvesting, Hampstead

food for the slaves. The ship had collected its cargo and had reached Tonga when the crew under Fletcher Christian mutinied. The crew claimed that Bligh's regime was too tyranical, and he and eighteen members of the crew who stayed loyal to him, were cast adrift in an open boat. The cargo of breadfruit was dumped overboard. Bligh, in a remarkable feat of seamanship, navigated the boat for 3,600 miles (5,796km) until making landfall on Timor in the East Indies. Some authorities have claimed that it was the breadfruit tree cargo that sparked the mutiny, as each morning the hundreds of trees in their heavy containers had to be carried on deck, and then carried down into the hold at nightfall. It might have proved just too much for the already overworked crew.

Whatever the reason for the mutiny, the breadfruit is a cheap carbohydrate-rich food, although pretty tasteless when boiled. It is best eaten fried, baked or roasted over charcoal. The slaves did not like them at first, but the tree spread and can now be found almost everywhere. It has large dark, green leaves, and the large green fruits can weigh 10 to 12lbs (4 to 5kgm). The falling fruits explode with a loud bang and splatter pulpy contents over a large distance. It is said that no one goes hungry when the breadfruit is in season.

Calabash trees are native to the Caribbean and have huge gourd like fruits which are very versatile when dried and cleaned. They can be used as water containers and bowls, bailers for boats, and as lanterns. Juice from the pulp is boiled into a concentrated syrup and used to treat coughs and colds, and the fruit is said to have many other medicinal uses. The calabash is St. Lucia's national tree.

Cocoa is another important crop, and its Latin name *theobroma* means 'food of the gods'. A cocoa tree can produce several thousand flowers a year, but only a fraction of these will develop into seed bearing pods. It is the heavy orange pods that hang from the cocoa tree which contain the beans which contain the seeds that produce cocoa and chocolate. The beans, containing a sweet, white sap that protects the seeds, are split open and kept in trays to ferment. This process takes up to 8 days and the seeds must be kept at a regular temperature to ensure the right flavour and aroma develops. The seeds are then dried. In the old days people used to walk barefoot over the beans to polish them to enhance their appearance. Today, the beans are crushed to extract cocoa butter, and the remaining powder is cocoa. Real chocolate is produced by mixing cocoa powder, cocoa butter and sugar.

You can buy cocoa balls, or rolls, like fat chocolate fingers in the markets which make a delicious drink. Each ball is the size of a large cherry. Simply dissolve the ball in a pan of boiling water, allow to simmer and then add sugar and milk or cream, for a rich chocolate drink. Each ball will make about four mugs of chocolate.

Coconut palms are everywhere and should be treated with caution. Anyone who has heard the 'whoosh' of a descending coconut, and leapt to safety, knows how scary the sound is. Very few people do get injured by falling coconuts which is a near miracle in view of the tens of thousands of palms all over the island. However it is not a good idea to picnic in a coconut grove!

Coconut trees are incredibly hardy, able to grow in sand and even when regularly washed by salty sea water. They can also survive long periods without rain.

Their huge leaves, up to 20ft (6m) long in mature trees, drop down during dry spells so a smaller surface area is exposed to the sun which reduces evaporation. Coconut palms can grow up to 80ft (24m) tall, and produce up to 100 seeds a year. The seeds are the second largest in the plant kingdom, and these fall when ripe.

The coconut traditionally bought in greengrocers, is the seed with its layer of coconut surrounded by a hard shell. This shell is then surrounded by a layer of copra, a fibrous material, and this is covered by a large green husk. The seed and protective coverings can weigh 30lb (13kgm) and more. The seed and casing is waterproof, drought proof and able to float, and this explains why coconut palms which originated in the Pacific and Indian Oceans, are now found throughout the Caribbean — the seeds literally floated across the seas.

The coconut palm is extremely versatile. The leaves can be used as thatch for roofing, or cut into strips and woven into mat and baskets, while the husks yield coir, a fibre resistant to salt water

Following pages: Golden Shower, growing in the Botanical Garden

and ideal for ropes and brushes and brooms. Green coconuts contain a delicious thirst-quenching 'milk', and the coconut 'meat' can be eaten raw, or baked in ovens for 2 days before being sent to processing plants where the oil is extracted. Coconut oil is used in cooking, soaps, synthetic rubber and even in hydraulic brake fluid.

As you drive around the island, you will see groups of men and women splitting the coconuts in half with machetes preparing them for the ovens. You might also see halved coconut shells spaced out on the corrugated tin roofs of some homes. These are being dried before being sold to the copra procressing plants.

Dasheen is one of the crops known as 'ground provisions' in the islands, the others being potatoes, yams, eddo and tannia. The last two are close relatives of dasheen, and all are members of the aroid family, some of the world's oldest cultivated crops. Dasheen with its 'elephant ear' leaves, and eddo grow from a corm which when boiled thoroughly can be used like potato, and the young leaves of either are used to make callaloo, a spinach-like soup. Both dasheen and eddo are thought to have come from China or Japan but

tannia is native to the Caribbean, and its roots can be boiled, baked or fried.

Guava is common throughout the islands, and the aromatic, pulpy fruit is also a favourite with birds who then distribute its seeds. The fruit bearing shrub can be seen on roadsides and in gardens, and it is used to make a wide range of products from jelly to 'cheese', a paste made by mixing the fruit with sugar. The fruit which ranges from a golf ball to a tennis ball in size, is a rich source of vitamin A and contains lots more vitamin C than citrus fruit.

Mango can be delicious if somewhat messy to eat. It originally came from India but is now grown throughout the Caribbean and found wherever there are people. Young mangoes can be stringy and unappetising, but ripe fruit from mature trees which grow up to 50ft (15m) and more, are usually delicious, and can be eaten raw or cooked. The juice is a great reviver in the morning, and the fruit is often used to make jams and other preserves. The wood of the mango is often used by boatbuilders.

Nutmeg trees are found on all the islands but Grenada is one of the world's top producers, although the price farmers get has crashed so much in recent years, that it is sometimes not economic to gather the crop. The tree thrives in hilly, wet areas and the fruit is the size of a small tomato. The outer husk, which splits open while still on the tree, is used to make the very popular nutmeg jelly. Inside the seed is protected by a bright red casing which when dried and crushed, produces the spice mace. Finally, the dark outer shell of the seed is broken open to reveal the nutmeg which is dried and then ground into a powder, or sold whole so that it can be grated to add flavour to dishes.

Passion fruit is not widely grown but it can usually be bought at the market. The pulpy fruit contains hundreds of tiny seeds, and many people prefer to press the fruit and drink the juice. It is also commonly used in fruit salads, sherbets and ice creams.

Pawpaw trees are also found throughout the island and are commonly grown in gardens. The trees are prolific fruit producers but grow so quickly that the fruit soon becomes difficult to gather. The large, juicy melon-like fruits are eaten fresh, pulped for juice or used locally to make jams, preserves and ice cream. They are rich sources of vitamin A and C. The leaves and fruit contain an enzyme which tenderises meat, and tough joints cooked wrapped in pawpaw leaves or covered in slices of fruit, usually taste like much more expensive cuts. The same enzyme, papain, is also used in chewing gum, cosmetics, the tanning industry and, somehow, in making wool shrink resistant. A tea made from unripe fruit is said to be good for lowering high blood pressure.

Pigeon peas are widely cultivated and can be found in many back gardens. The plants are very hardy and drought resistant, and are prolific yields of peas which can be eaten fresh or dried and used in soups and stews.

Pineapples were certainly grown in the Caribbean by the time Columbus arrived, and were probably brought from South America by the Amerindians. The fruit is slightly smaller than the Pacific pineapple, but the flavour more intense.

Sugar apple is a member of the annona fruit family, and grows wild and in gardens throughout the islands. The small, soft sugar apple fruit can be peeled off in strips when ripe, and is like eating thick apple sauce. They are eaten fresh or used to make sherbet or

Following pages: Parrot House in the Botanical Garden with two types of endangered birds

WELCOME
TO THE
DOMINICA PARROT AVIARY

SISSEROU
(AMAZONA IMPERIALIS)

JACO
(AMAZONA ARAUSIACA)

THIS AVIARY WAS BUILT IN AN ATTEMPT TO PREVENT THE EXTINCTION
OF OUR TWO ENDEMIC PARROTS, THE JACO AND THE SISSEROU.
THE GOVERNMENT OF DOMINICA IS GRATEFUL TO THE JERSEY WILDLIFE PRESERVATION
TRUST AND ALL OTHER CONTRIBUTORS.

drinks. Soursop, is a member of the same family, and its spiny fruits can be seen in hedgerows and gardens. They are eaten fresh or used for preserves, drinks and ice cream.

Sugar cane is grown for making rum and canes can grow up to 12ft (4m) tall and after cutting, the canes have to be crushed to extract the sugary juice. Most estates had their own sugar mill powered by water wheels or windmills. The remains of many of these mills can still be seen around the island, and much of the original machinery, mostly made in Britain, is still in place. After extraction, the juice is boiled until the sugar crystalises. The mixture remaining is molasses and this is used to produce rum.

FOOD AND DRINK

Food

Dining out in the Caribbean offers the chance to experiment with all sorts of unusual spices, vegetables and fruits, with creole and island dishes, and, of course, rum punches and other exotic cocktails.

Dominican cuisine is largely a blend of French and Creole, and the secret to its success is in the preparation of the ingredients,

particularly their spicing or marination. Dominican cooks have the added advantage that they have access at almost all times to the freshest ingredients, and they are experts at the subtle blending of herbs and spices.

Eating out is generally very relaxed, and few restaurants have a strict dress code, although most people like to wear something a little smarter at dinner after a day on the beach or out sightseeing.

Many hotels have a tendency to offer buffet dinners or barbecues, but even these can be interesting and tasty affairs.

Breakfast can be one of the most exciting meals of the day for a visitor. There is a huge range of fruit juices to choose from. Try a glass of water melon juice, followed by a fresh grapefruit, or slices of chilled pawpaw or mango. Most hotels offer fruit plates offering a wide choice so you should be able to taste your way through them all during your stay.

The island's fruits also make great jams and preserves, and you can follow the fruit with piping hot toast spread with perhaps citrus marmalade or guava jam, washed down with the island's own coffee.

Lunches are best eaten at beach cafés which usually offer excellent barbecued fresh fish and conch — which often appears on menus as lambi (not to be confused with lamb). Lobster and crab are also widely available. Dishes are mostly served with local vegetables such as fried plantain, cassava and yam, and fresh fruit such as pineapple, mango, golden apple or papaya, makes an ideal and light dessert. There is a steady supply of fruit through the year as different varieties have different seasons. During the summer, there are fruits such as the kenip, plumrose, sugar apple and yellow plum. Green bananas and plantains are usually eaten raw, or boiled or steamed in the skin, then cut into slices and served very hot. They also make excellent chips when fried.

There is an enormous choice when it comes to dinner.

Starters include a huge choice of locally grown and produced fruit juices from orange and grapefruit to the more unusual ones like soursop and tamarind. You can also drink green coconut 'milk'.

Traditional Caribbean starters include dishes such as Christophene and coconut soup, and callaloo soup made from the young leaves of dasheen, a

spinach like vegetable. The soup is made throughout the Caribbean and in Dominica, ochroes, smoked meat and sometimes crab are added, as well as lots of herbs and spices.

There is also a strong French tradition with such dishes as soupe Germou made from pumpkin and garlic, and pouile dudon, a chicken stew with coconut and molasses. Fish and clam chowders are also popular starters. Try heart of palm, excellent fresh shrimps or scallops, smoked kingfish wrapped in crepes or crab backs, succulent land crab meat sauteed with breadcrumbs and seasoning, and served restuffed in the shell. It is much sweeter than the meat of sea crabs.

The fish is generally excellent, and do not be alarmed if you see dolphin on the menu. It is not the protected species made famous by 'Flipper', but a solid, close-textured flat faced fish called the dorado, which is delicious. There is also snapper, kingfish, redfish, jacks, balaouy, snapper, tuna, flying fish, lobster, swordfish, baby squid and and mussels. Delicious river crayfish are usually caught at night.

Following pages: Calabash tree

CARIBBEAN SUNSEEKERS: DOMINICA

Try seafood jambalaya, chunks of lobster, shrimps and ham served on a bed of braised seasoned rice, shrimp Creole, with fresh shrimp sauted in garlic butter and parsley and served with tomatoes, or fish Creole, with fresh fish steaks cooked in a spicy onion, garlic and tomato sauce and served with rice and fried plaintain. Other island dishes may include sauted scallops with ginger, curried fish steaks lightly fried with a curry sauce and served with sliced bananas, cucumber, fresh coconut and rice.

It seems such a waste to travel to the Caribbean and eat burgers and steaks, especially when there are many much more exciting meat dishes available.

You could try curried chicken served in a coconut shell, oven baked chicken with pineapple and mango, curried goat served with freshly grated coconut, gingered chicken with mango and spices or Caribbean souse, with cuts of lean pork marinated with shredded cucumber, onions, garlic, lime juice and pepper sauce. Another island speciality is crapaud or mountain chicken — delicious frogs' legs. There is also highly seasoned black pudding.

For vegetarians there are excellent salads, stuffed breadfruit, callaloo bake, stuffed squash and pawpaw, baked

sweet potato and yam casserole.

For dessert, try fresh fruit salad, with added cherry juice, and sometimes a little rum, which is a year round popular dessert.

Or, try one of the exotically flavoured ice creams. There are also banana fritters and banana flambe, coconut cheesecake and tropical fruit sorbets.

Most menus and dishes are self explanatory, but one or two things are worth bearing in mind. When green fig appears on the menu, it usually means green banana, which is peeled and boiled as a vegetable. Salt fish used to be salted cod, but now it can be any fish.

On the buffet table, you will often see a dish called pepper pot. This is usually a hot, spicy meat and vegetable stew to which may be added small flour dumplings and shrimps.

There are wonderful breads in the Caribbean, and you should try them if you get the chance. There are banana and pumpkin breads, and delicious cakes such as coconut loaf cake, guava jelly cookies and rum cake.

Do not be afraid to eat out. Food is often preapred in front of you, and there are some great snacks available from island eateries. Try deep fried cakes of dough called floats, or saltfish or corned beef fritters, or coconut patties.

You must try roti, an East Indian creation, which is available almost everywhere. It is a paper thin dough wrapped round a spicy, hot curry mixture, and contains beef, chicken, vegetables or fish. The chicken roti often contains bones which some people like to chew on, so be warned.

Drink

Rum is the Caribbean drink. There are almost as many rums in the West Indies as their are malt whiskies in Scotland (Britain), and there is an amazing variety of strength, colour and quality. The finest rums are best drunk on the rocks, but if you want to capture a bit of the Caribbean spirit, have a couple of rum punches.

To make Plantation Rum Punch, thoroughly mix 3 ounces of rum, with 1 ounce of lime juice and one teaspoon of honey, then pour over crushed ice, and add a pinch of freshly grated nutmeg.

Most hotels and bars also offer a wide range of cocktails both alcoholic, usually very strong, and non-alcoholic. Beer, drunk cold and from the bottle, is the most popular drink, and wine, where available, is often expensive because of taxes, and the choice limited.

Tap water is safe to drink as are ice cubes made from it. Mineral and bottled water is widely available, as are soft drinks.

Note: While many of the restaurants do offer excellent service, time does not always have the same urgency as it does back home, and why should it? After all, as you are on holiday, relax, enjoy a drink, the company and the surroundings and do not worry if things take just a little longer, the wait is generally worth it.

Touring & Exploring Dominica

GETTING AROUND DOMINICA

Getting around is easy and part of the adventure of taking a vacation on Dominica. In the past, however, heavy rains frequently washed away the roads. It was not until 1956 that the first road across the island was completed, and a major road building programme to improve communications did not really get under way until the mid 1980s.

There are now around 470 miles (757km) of roads on the island, of which around 300 miles (482km) are paved, although conditions are obviously not as good off main roads. Virtually all parts of the island though are now accessible by road, even if the last leg of the journey, to a secluded beach perhaps, has to be made on foot. Care needs to be taken driving anywhere on the island for several reasons. The scenery is so stunning that people are often concentrating more on the views than

The Layou River estuary runs down the side of the main coast road

the road; after rain there can be landslips and debris on the road; and, it is quite common to drive round a corner and find youself in the middle of a cricket match because the reasonably flat surface makes a great wicket! Expect far more potholes than at home too. Your car insurance may not cover unpaved roads.

Taxis and mini buses for hire can be recognised by registration numbers starting with the letter 'H'. There are set fares for most trips by taxi and mini-bus but it is always a good idea to agree on the price and the currency it is being quoted in, before setting off.

Taxis: There are plenty of taxis at both airports and in Roseau during the day. There are fewer taxis operating after 6pm and it is advisable to book in advance if you are planning an evening trip. Some sample fares are from Canefield Airport to Roseau EC$20, Canefield to Portsmouth EC$110, Canefield Airport to Soufrière EC$60, and from Melville Hall Airport to Roseau EC$45, Melville Airport to Portsmouth EC$30.

Taxis hired for tours and sightseeing usually charge around EC$45 an hour for up to 4 passengers.

Mini buses: Mini buses are the fun and cheap way of travelling around the island, and give you the chance to get to know the islanders if you can hear what they are saying over the blaring music that normally accompanies every trip.

Buses: You can catch buses for Trafalgar and the Roseau Valley from Valley Road near the police headquarters. Buses for Soufrière and the south leave from the Old Market; for the west and north from near the new market close to West Bridge; and for the east from Queen Mary Street.

Typical fares are Roseau to: Salisbury EC$3.50, Portsmouth EC$7.50 and Canefield EC$1.50.

By Air: Both LIAT and Air Guadeloupe operate special day tours, and Carribean Air Services is available for charters.

By Boat: Fishing boats can be hired for sea sightseeing and fishing trips, and diving centres also organise tours.

ROSEAU

* Roseau is a busy, colourful little town that is a hive of activity and honking traffic during the day, and very quiet at night unless you know where to go for entertainment.

It is a strange mix of old and new, faded and smart. The waterfront area has been considerably smartened up and makes a delightful place to stroll during the day or evening. The oldest part of town, around Old Market Square, has several interesting old buildings which fortunately survived Hurricane David in 1979, and the newer part of the town, just south of the Roseau River, has offices and shops and bazaars whose wares often spill out onto the sidewalks.

Roseau is the island's capital, has about a quarter of the island's population and is the only large town on Dominica. It gets its name from the French word for 'reed', because these were growing so profusely in the mouth of the river. The river used to flood regularly and in 1806 it overflowed its banks and flooded the town, claiming the lives of more than 130 people.

Over the years, Roseau has seen its share of disasters. It has been bombarded on several occasions, burnt down twice and suffered many other serious fires over the last 200 years. It has also been hit by hurricanes ten times since 1781.

The best way of seeing Roseau is to walk around it. It is a compact capital and has lots of secret places that would be missed if you drove round.

There are many fine old buildings, including some interesting churches. Many of the oldest buildings are made of stone and wood and have the elaborate fretwork ornamentation known as gingerbread, which is found throughout the Caribbean on balconies and under eaves. There are also wrought iron balconies, and louvred shutters known as jalousies. These shutters have slats which can be opened or closed to control the amount of light and air, and the word 'jalousie' comes from the French for jealousy, presumably because when adjusted properly, one could look out and see what was going on without being seen. One of the finest buildings is La Robe Creole Restaurant in Fort Street, a classic stone building of West Indian architecture with its arched doors and windows. During the rebuilding following Hurricane David, many of the older Creole buildings were restored to their former conditions, while most of the new construction was a mixture of concrete and wood.

There is a mix of architecure to be seen in Roseau, and some of the older buildings have thick stone walls and elaborate brickwork. The Fort Young Hotel, for instance, used to be the town's main fortification, thus its name. The old warehouses and many of the homes are built on stone foundations with a wooden upper floor, complete with overhanging balcony over the pavements.

The town lies to the south of the Roseau River and there has been a lot of building in the last few years not only to repair damage caused by Hurricane David, but to improve facilities for tourists and the appearance of the waterfront area between the river mouth and south to the Fort Young Hotel area. This waterfront area, Roseau's promenade, is now called the **Bay Front**, and was officially opened on 9 August 1993. The Roseau Seawall and

Bayfront Development Project involved building a new seawall 60ft (18m) beyond the Bayfront. The wall is designed to reduce the impact of storm seas in future hurricanes, but it has also greatly enhanced the waterfront area. Its construction allowed land in front of the sea wall to be reclaimed and this area has now been landscaped with footpaths, ornate street lighting and benches. The construction also involved the rebuilding of the old Roseau Jetty, also destroyed by the hurricane in 1979. The new jetty has improved facilities for visiting yachts and other small craft.

The second phase of this development project is already under way and includes the new Cruise Ship Berth beyond the sea wall, which opened in June 1995, while the old Post Office is being renovated to house the Division of Tourism. It will also include public toilets, and a reception area for cruise passengers and other tourists to the town. A craft and souvenir market within the Old Market is also planned, together with a new ferry passenger terminal on the new Roseau jetty.

Before Hurricane David most telephone and power lines were above ground, and one benefit of the reconstruction is that many of

Potters Ville

National Development Corporation and Division of Tourism Head Office

Roseau River

Government Headquarters

Windsor Park

AID Bank and National * Commercial Bank

Roseau River

Alliance Francaise of Dominica *

MORN BRUC

Banque Français Commerciale

Fire and *Police HQ

Bank of Nova Scotia *

Botanical Gardens *

Market *

*LIAT

Cable and Wireless * Telephone Services

Dominica Hotel Association

Forestry and *National Parks Office

Infirmary

Post Office *

Barclays Bank PLC

R.C. Cathedral

Court House

Dominica Tourist Information

Methodist Church

Royal Bank of Canada *

R.C. Cemetery *

*Government Cemetery

KING HILL

Old Market *

Anglican Church

Peebles Park

State House

Fort Young

Library

*Old Court House

Radio Station *

House of Assembly

*Anglican Cemetery

CHARLOTT VALLEY

N
W — E
S

Charlotte Ville

0   1/16   1/8   3/16   4/16 mile

0   100   200   300 metres

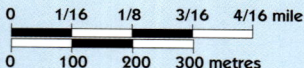

these have now been relocated underground, or camouflaged by landscaping.

* The **market**, as with all Caribbean towns, is where everything seems to happen during the day. It is at the northern end of the Bay Front on the corner with River Bank and close to the river's estuary. While there are stalls and a covered area, many of the islanders prefer to spread their produce on a mat on the ground, shading it from the sun by large umbrellas. The sight of the islanders in their brightly coloured costumes, the assortment of fruit and vegetables, and an array of multi-coloured golf umbrellas, all adds to the excitement of your visit to the market. The old market, which was also the location for public executions, was close to Fort Young and has now been re-

vamped as Dawbiney Market Plaza. The market was moved to its present location in 1972.

If you walk down the Bay Front, you pass the **old Post Office**, originally the Market House built in 1810, and the new Court House and Registry to the **Old Market**, formerly the slave market, which stands in a square at the seaward end of King George V Street. In 1895 a Dominican philanthropist left £500 for a covered building to be erected in the square and this now houses handicrafts stalls and a small café. The nearby **Peebles Park** has a bandstand, and benches where you can sit and watch the world go by.

The **Cable & Wireless offices** are in Old Street, a couple of streets inland from the Post Office, and **Barclays Bank** is a little further down the street.

The northern half of the town is laid out in grid style drawn up in the 1760s after the British took over the island, with a modern one way system to control traffic over the river. Vehicles entering the town from the north cross the bridge which leads into Queen Mary Street, while traffic leaving Roseau cross the bridge opposite Great George Street. **Government Headquarters** are at the top of Kennedy Street, and the **Fire and Police Headquarters** are at the corner of Bath Road and King George V Street. There are health centres on Hillsborough Street. Novelist Jean Rhys was born in Cork Street in what is now Vena's Guest House.

The area south of the Old Market, which was the heart of the first settlement, is a maze of small, narrow streets. Between Virgin and Turkey Lanes there are the **Methodist Church** alongside the near Gothic-Romanesque Roman Catholic **Cathedral of Our Lady of the Assumption** consecrated in 1841. It has a pleasing aspect because of its contrasting coloured volcanic stones, and its very construction is a tribute to the faith of its congregation. Although the vast majority of the islanders were and still are Catholic, the colony was officially Anglican and refused to help finance the cathedral's construction, so after working during the day, the congregation would work at night gathering stones from along the Roseau river for the building. Although it was consecrated in 1841 it was not until 1916 that building finished

Preceding page: Roseau Market

with the completion of the west steeple. The church has a beautiful and historic interior. The pulpit is reputed to have been donated by prisoners on Devil's Island.

The **St. George's Anglican Church**, built in Regency style in 1820 and enlarged in the early part of the twentieth century, was completely destroyed by Hurricane David, and was hit again during rebuilding. It is just inland from the Fort Young Hotel, south of Turkey Lane, and across the road, set in fine grounds is the revamped brilliantly white **State House** with the **House of Assembly** just south on Victoria Street. Until independence, State House was the official residence of the Governor, and it is now used for state receptions and similar functions.

Fort Young was built between 1700 and 1783 to protect the sea approaches after it was decided that Roseau rather than Portsmouth should be the main town of the island. It was heavily fortified with very thick walls, and these now help keep the interior very cool when it is blisteringly hot outside. It opened as a hotel in 1964. The flagstones in the shaded

courtyard are the original stones laid, and some of the former armaments can still be seen dotted around the hotel and its grounds. Opposite, on the beach side of the road are the library and radio station. The **library** was built in 1902 with a grant from the Carnegie Foundation, and used to be surrounded by public gardens. A canon ball tree near Fort Young was one of the garden's original specimens. The library is worth visiting if you want to learn more about the island because it has books on every aspect of Dominica.

The Cenotaph is in Victoria Street, and further along are the ruins of the Georgian **Old Court House** built in 1811, but burnt during during unrest in 1979.

If you take Turkey Lane inland past the Roman Catholic Cathedral, you reach Queen Mary Street. Turn right past the infirmary, and then cross over Bath Road for the Botanical Gardens, Forestry and National Parks Office and Plant Nursery. Windsor Park, the main sporting venue, lies to the south of the Roseau River.

The **Botanical Gardens** are on the outskirts of Roseau at the foot of the Morne Bruce Hill, worth

Following pages: Roseau Market Hall, and the Library (inset)

walking up for the great views from the top close to the large Crucifix and shrine erected in 1924. You can walk up by taking Jacks Walk from the Botanical Gardens, or you can drive. There used to be British garrison stationed on the summit and the buildings were designed by a Royal Engineer James Bruce, whose name it now carries.

There are two entrances to the gardens, the Main Gate or North Gate is of Valley Road, and the Roseau Gate is off Bath Road. The rolling gardens and lawns cover 40 acres (16 hectares), and comprise the largest area of open space within the city. Although only 66ft (20m) above sea level, the gardens get around 85 inches (212cm) of rain a year which helps to account for the lush vegetation and prolific growth of so many species.

The gardens are on the site of a former sugar cane plantation, and were landscaped and planted in 1890. They were planned in two sections, an ornamental area and an economic one which concentrated on growing and propogating plants of commercial importance. For many decades they were considered among the finest botanical gardens in the Caribbean, especially the ornamental gardens with their

lakes and fountain, and around 500 species of flowers, shrubs and trees, including almost 100 different types of palm.

While perhaps not in their original glory, the gardens have survived remarkably, especially in view of tropical storms and hurricanes, although they were badly hit by Hurricane David in 1979 which lashed the grounds for 8 hours. The force of the hurricane can be gauged by the crushed bus lying under the huge Baobab tree which was uprooted by the storm.

In the 1960s and 1970s, the gardens also became a popular cricket venue, and Queen Elizabeth accompanied by Prince Phillip, have twice visited the grounds. They are still used today for some cricket matches and official ceremonies.

There are almost fifty species of trees from around the world, including the sausage tree and African tulip from West Africa, and the orchid tree from South East Asia, and many beautiful flowering shrubs such as the oleander, bougainvillea and ixora.

The Forestry and Wildlife Division has produced a pamphlet *A Guide to Selected Trees and Shrubs* which has a location map of the gardens identifying the different trees and shrubs which can be seen.

The aviary in the gardens is important because it is used as a breeding station for the island's two parrots, the Jaco and the Sisserou, both of which are endangered species. The aviary has two exhibition cages which can be visited by the public, while out of sight are the breeding cages and utility and research area. The Forestry Division also runs the highly successful Sisserou Express, a converted coach which is a travelling exhibition and educational facility aimed at schools and rural communities.

Close to the Botanical Gardens in Elmshall Road is the **Alliance Francaise of Dominica**, part of a worldwide network run by a non-profit making Dominican organisation, which aims to teach the French language and establish cultural ties. The Alliance Francaise is open to the public, and offers French classes for all ages and levels of ability. It also has a library and a small theatre. It is open weekdays between 9am and 12noon and 2pm and 7pm (☎ 448-6008).

Immediately across the bridges over the Roseau River, is the

suburb of **Potters Ville**, with **Goodwill** running on from it to the north along the coast, and just inland of both is **Limefields**. The Princess Margaret Hospital is in Goodwill, and the island's teacher training college is in Limefields.

EATING OUT IN ROSEAU

Inexpensive	$
Moderate	$$
Expensive	$$$

Blue Max Cafe and Deli $
16 Hanover Street ☎ 449-8907. A café offering snacks, deli style sandwiches and excellent coffee.

Callaloo Restaurant $-$$
66 King George V Street ☎ 448-3386. A great Caribbean restaurant, specialising in traditional island dishes such as Callaloo soup, Crapaud, lobster and crayfish. Ingredients are always fresh so the menu reflects what is available. Open Monday to Saturday 7.30am-10pm.

Cartwheel Cafe $
Bay Street ☎ 448-5353.

Following page: Roseau Botanical Garden

On the Bay Front and offering snacks and lunches.

Continental Inn $-$$
37 Queen Mary Street
☎ 448-2214. A small and friendly restaurant offering Creole cuisine.

Creole Kitchen $-$$
Woodstone Mall, Cork Street
☎ 448-6052. Good creole cooking at very affordable prices.

Evergreen Hotel $-$$ Castle Comfort, ☎ 448-3288. The Crystal Terrace restaurant set in a tropical garden, specialises in local cuisine.

Fort Young Hotel $$-$$$
Victoria Street ☎ 448-5000.
A very good restaurant offering a la carte Creole and international dishes in an historic setting. Buffet dinners are offered regularly and provide the chance to taste island specialities. There is also a reasonable wine list.

The Garraway Hotel $$-$$$
Bay Front ☎ 449-8800.
The restaurant with its fine views offers a wide choice of food from quick snacks to full meals featuring traditional Creole and International dishes.

Green Parrot $ 10 Bay Front
☎ 448-8944.
Offers snacks and light meals.

Guiyave Restaurant and Bar $-$$
15 Cork Street ☎ 448-2930. Dine in style on the balcony of this old town house. The restaurant is rightly popular and serves good, local dishes.

Kent Anthony Guest House $
3 Great Marlborough Street
☎ 448-2730. The restaurant is open to the public and offers local cuisine at very affordable prices.

La Robe Creole $-$$
Fort Street ☎ 448-2896.
On the Bay Front opposite Peebles Park, air conditioned and offering a snack menu as well as excellent a la carte Creole dishes. Friendly and attentive service by staff dressed in traditional island costume, thus the restaurant's name.

La Tropicale $-$$
15 King George V Street
☎ 448-3772.

Preceding page: Four different palms trees in the Botanical Garden (above)
Balconied properties are a common sight in Roseau (below)

Mange Dominique $-$$ $
Cork Street ☎ 448-7100.

Margheritia's Pizzeria $
10 Old Street ☎ 448-6003.
More than just a pizzeria with
excellent cheesecake, pastries
and ice cream.

Mousehole $
Fort Street ☎ 448-2896.
Tasty snacks in the basement of La
Robe Creole Restaurant.

Orchard Restaurant $-$$
Corner of King George V and Great
George Streets ☎ 448-3051. A great
place for a snack or traditional
Creole meal with lambi, goat,
chicken or fish. There are also
vegetarian dishes usually available.
Try the roti and black pudding.
Open Monday to Friday 8am-
10pm, and Saturday 8am-4pm.

Paiho Restaurant $-$$
10 Church Street ☎ 448-8999.
The island's first Chinese restaurant
specialising in Hunan style country
cooking. Take away is available.

Pearl's Cuisine $
19 Castle Street ☎ 448-8707.
Excellent local cuisine, especially
fresh fish, shrimp and chicken.

Open from breakfast to dinner for
eat in or take out. There is usually
a very good value set three course
lunch and dinner

Pina Colada Bar $
30 Bath Road ☎ 448-6921.
Offers snacks, light meals and
drinks and evening entertainment.

Pizza Palace $
River Bank ☎ 448-4598.
Fast food outlet offering pizzas,
other snacks and soft drinks.

Raffoul Snackette $
13 King George V Street
☎ 448-4145. Great for a quick
snack of pattie and fruit juice at
lunchtime or during the day.

Trends $-$$
Hillsorough Street. Snacks, light
meals and drinks, and evening
entertainment.

World of Food $-$$
Queen Mary Street
☎ 448-3286. A popular restuarant
for lunch and dinner where you
can dine in the courtyard shaded
by the large mango tree.

*Following pages: The sulphur spring that lies at the end of an unmade road inland
from Soufrière*

EATING OUT AROUND ROSEAU

Castaways Beach Restaurant $$-$$$
Castaways Hotel, Mero
☎ 449-6244. Fine dining in the Almond Terrace Restaurant which serves Creole and continental dishes.

Evergreen Hotel $$
Castle Comfort ☎ 448-3288. The small restaurant specialises in local cuisine.

Gachette's Seaside Restaurant $$
Scott's Head ☎ 448-4551. Some of the best fish on the island, and not surprising as it is fresh and caught locally.

Good Times Restaurant $-$$
Checkhall ☎ 449-1660. Snacks and drinks available and a fun place in the evenings.

Lauro Club $$
Salisbury ☎ 449-6602. The restaurant, perched on the cliffs, is noted for its local cuisine, especially fish and shrimp.

Layou River Hotel $$
Layou ☎ 449-6081. The award winning terrace restaurant specialises in local Creole and authentic Chinese cooking.

Ocean Terrace $$
Anchorage Hotel, Castle Comfort
☎ 448-2638. The restaurant offers a choice of local Creole specialities and International dishes.

Papillote Wilderness Retreat $$
Trafalgar Falls Road ☎ 448-2287. This recently renovated restaurant is set in tropical gardens and beside a natural hot mineral pool. It serves local Creole dishes, health-food oriented dishes and a variety of Caribbean and International foods.

Reigate Hall Hotel $-$$
Reigate ☎ 448-4031. Enjoy traditional Creole and International cuisine in the hotel's unique hanging restaurant.

River Side Cuisine $-$$
Loubiere ☎ 448-6447. Local dishes.

Seamoons Club $-$$
Massacre ☎ 449-1061. Snacks and local dishes.

Shipwreck $-$$
Donkey Beach, Canefield
☎ 449-1059. Snacks and local dishes and specialising in fish.

Tony's Corner $-$$ Mero. Snacks and local dishes available.

THE SOUTH

The tour heads south from Roseau along the coast through the suburbs of Charlotteville and Castle Comfort with its sprinkling of hotels to Loubiere, where the road divides.

INLAND FROM LOUBIERE

The inland road is very steep and climbs over the mountain before descending to the sea at historic **Bereuka** on **Grand Bay**. In the mountains at **Bellevue Chopin** you can take a walking detour north to **Morne Anglais**.

This area was the home of some of the island's largest plantations and it is still predominantly agricultural, producing citrus fruits, especially grapefruit.

The great sweep of Grand Bay was protected by forts on the headlands at Carib Point and Pointe Tanama, and remains of fortifications can still be seen along the cliffs.

The church in the village of **Grand Bay** with its steep streets, has interesting local scenes painted over the days and fearsome looking gargoyles sticking out from the roof. The crucifix in the cemetery is the oldest on the island and was carved from a solid piece of stone around 1720. The church's bell tower was relocated in the hills, so that its peals could be heard over a wider area.

From Berekua you can take the road west to visit the **Soufrière Sulphur Springs** above the village of Soufrière, but these are best visited from the village itself.

Our road then continues around the coast to **Fond Saint Jean** and **Petite Savane**. There are the remains of old sugar mills at **Geneva** and **Stowe**, and at **Bagatelle** close to Fond Saint Jean.

The area around Petite Savane, a village with strong French traditions, is a centre for bay oil production and there are a number of small distilleries giving off their sweet aromas.

Take a look at the cricket pitch as well which is perched on the

Following page: Soufrière

Nature Island Dive
BA DIVING
SNORKELING
UNTAIN BIKING
AKING   ISLAND TOURS
4498181   FAX 4498182

Soufrière Bay (above)
Scots Head in silhouette at the end of the day from Soufrière

cliff. Any boundaries hit that way go straight over the edge into the sea.

Because of the steep mountains which plunge straight into the sea at this point, the road ends at Petite Savane, but there is a path inland which runs parallel with the coast and then runs down to the sea at Pointe Mulatre.

SOUTH FROM LOUBIERE

If you continue south at Loubiere rather than drive inland, you can follow the coast road down beneath the towering **cliffs of Solomon**, scene of fierce fighting between the British and French in 1778, past **Pointe Michel** and **Pointe Guignard**. The road runs inland for a short way round **Morne la Sorcier**, where allegedly Caribs threw unfaithful wives to their deaths, and then back to the coast and Soufrière. This whole stretch of coastline was very heavily fortified and you can wander round the ruins of Fort Cachacrou on Scotts Head.

Soufrière is a friendly little village, and was one of the first places on the island to be settled. The first French settlers named it after the sulphur which belches from the ground a little way up the valley. The church, noted for its murals of village life, is by the beach with boats and palm trees alongside and with the forest behind always threatening to engulf it.

Soufrière also used to be the location of the famous Rose's Lime Juice factory. Limes grown all round the island were hauled or shipped to the factory for pressing and processing and at one time, sales of lime juice abroad accounted for one half of all the island's export income. You can visit the ruins of the lime press and the old sugar cane mills. Today the area is noted for the production of aloe.

Soufrière is also noted for its jump-ups, or street party festivals called Korne Korn La, during which there is a lot of singing and dancing, and a fair amount of eating and drinking.

You can drive along the unmade road or walk up the Soufrière River Valley to visit the **Soufrière Sulphur Springs** and the hot water pools. The French built baths here for their soldiers. Along the river there are huge stands of towering bamboo, and the villagers take advantage of the hot water for bathing and washing their clothes. The water temperature can vary from hot to very hot, so check it out before plunging in.

Scotts Head on the south-western tip of the island used to be dominated by **Fort Cachacrou**, but the fortification is now in ruins. The fort gets its name from the Carib word 'cashachou' which is the name they originally gave the headland. It means 'that which is being eaten by the sea'. Scott was one of the British officers who helped capture the island from the French in 1761. Over the centuries it has seen lots of action. In 1778 during the American War of Independence, the French General de Bouillé landed his invasion force close to the fort which was quickly captured, and he then went on to capture the whole island.

The fort commands an imposing position with wonderful views across the Martinique Channel to the French island 20 miles (32km) to the south, and with views northwards along the western coast to Roseau and beyond. You can also look leeward to view the Caribbean and windward to see the Atlantic, and you can see the different colours of the sea where the two meet.

The area between Scotts Head and Soufrière is now a protected marine reserve, and an example of how the environment can be protected alongside the needs of tourism and the traditional activities of locals. A marine reserve differs from a marine park, because it not only seeks to protect the environment, but also aims to cater for recreational needs and maintain traditional economic activities and encourage new ones. The reserve extends from Point Cachacrou in the south to Anse Bateaux in the north, and it includes all the coastal area in between, although it has been divided into zones to accommodate the different activities allowed — fishing, swimming, snorkelling and scuba diving. The reserve is ideal for both novice and experienced divers, snorkellers and swimmers. For those who do not want to get wet, the area is great for artists, photographers, picnickers and sunbathers.

Note: Soufrière Bay is also famed for the phenomenon known as a white squall, caused by winds which every so often comes powering down the steep leeward mountain side. As the winds hit the water, they cause a swell which then races out to sea until it is dissipated, but woe betide any yachts or small boats in its path.

Having visited Scotts Head the only way back to Roseau is to retrace your route north along the same coast road.

TOUR AND EXPLORE DOMINICA WITH RON MELLOW

The best way of discovering more about the Native Island is a guide for the day. Ron Mellow will cater for all your requirements — whether you want a hike up to the Boiling Lake, a general tour of the island, visit the waterfalls, swim in natural hot springs or spend a lazy afternoon picnicing by and swimming in the Layou River.

It is best if you do not try to walk any of the trails without a guide. It is not only more interesting but also more prudent up in the rain forest and over rough terrain.

Dominica has many hidden treasures which only a guide can help you discover. A list of recommended guides can be found on page 152. Ron Mellow can be contacted at PO Box 48, Roseau, Dominica ☎ 1 809 449 8026.

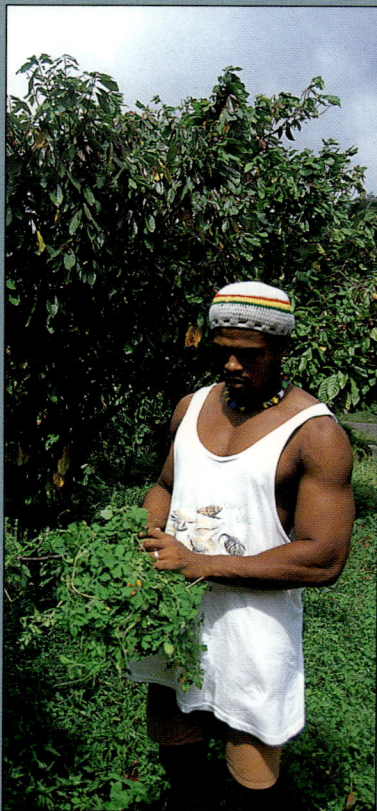

Ron Mellow picking Pomme Couli, which he uses to make a 'tea' to purify blood

TRAFALGAR FALLS
DANGER

THE INTERIOR FROM ROSEAU

There are no trans-island routes in the southern third of the island, but there are a number of roads which provide access into the interior and the spectacular **Morne Trois Pitons National Park**. This is an area that is best explored on foot and there are great trails and nature walks. Always wear stout, non-slip footwear and carry raingear and a warm jumper, because it can be chilly if the sun is hidden and the winds get up. A guide is strongly recommended not only to ensure you find the right trails, but also to make certain you do not miss all the things to see and do along the way.

The park was the first nature reserve in the Caribbean and contains many of Dominica's most spectacular natural attractions. Many of these attractions can only be reached by a hike although some sights can be reached by car.

The easiest trip is to **Trafalgar Falls** and is accessed by taking the road which is the extension of King George V Street, which crosses the Roseau River and then continues through Bath Estate for just under 5 miles (8km) to where the trail for the falls starts from the road. At Ford Cani take the left fork for the falls and Laudat, and then after about 1 mile (2km) take the right hand fork which leads to the falls.

The falls are reached after a 15 minute walk along a good well marked trail although there is a little scrambling through the rocks beyond the viewpoint, and the rocks are slippery in places. There are two falls splashing down through a gorge into pools littered with huge black rocks, and surrounded by lush vegetation, especially ferns and orchids. The larger of the falls on the left is called the 'Father', and the smaller one 'Mother'. The flow of the smaller waterfall is reduced considerably during the dry season, and the flow of both is less than it used to be because the falls have been harnessed to provide hyrdro electric power. You can see the pipes which carry the water to the turbines in the generating station. Take your swimming costume and wear

Preceding page: Trafalgar Falls, showing the left hand fall

non-slip footwear as the rocks can be tricky. You can climb up along the left of the 'Father' fall side and halfway up 'Father' there is a hot pool you can relax in. Do not climb up the middle of the falls. The red oxide staining marks the flow of the hot water.

Close to the falls is the **Papillote Wilderness Retreat and Nature Sanctuary**, which includes a hotel and good restaurant, set in fabulous tropical gardens, with hot mineral pools, waterfalls, fountains and paths through heavily scented flowers. It is an oasis in the rain forest, and has deservedly won eco-awards for its sensitive development.

The **Wotten Waven Sulphur Springs** are across the valley from the falls. There are mineral rich hot water pools and bubbling mud pools, both reputed to have therapeutic properties, and both are reminders of the island's volcanic past. The sulphur laden air is also said to be healthy and you can sit in the pools, but test the temperature of the water first.

Morne Trois Pitons National Park covers 17,000 (6,800 hectares) acres of primordial rain forest, and contains the Titou Gorge, Boeri

and Freshwater Crater Lakes, Bubbling Lake and the Middleham Falls just to the north-west of Laudat, which is the best access point. All these natural attractions can be reached by trails. Again, take the same road out of Roseau and head for Trafalgar Falls but take the left hand turning for Laudat when the road forks. The idea for the park was first put forward in 1952 but it was not until funding became available in 1973 that the idea could progress, and the park was officially designated in 1975 with the enactment of the National Parks and Protected Areas Act. You are recommended to take a guide on all the trails listed.

If you are heading for Freshwater Lake, you can drive in a four wheel drive vehicle a couple of miles beyond Laudat for the trail, otherwise you have to walk the 2½ miles (4km) there along an old carriage road from the Laudat shrine.

The 9 acre (4 hectare) **Freshwater Lake**, the largest in Dominica, stands at 2,500ft (762m) above sea level, and the road to it runs round the southern edge of Morne Macaque. The

Following pages: Trafalgar village with Trafalgar Falls showing the right hand fall (inset)

lake, the source of the Roseau River, has been tapped to augment the island's hydro-electric power supplies. The lake also supports a lot of wildlife and there are great views of the eastern coastline from this beautiful vantage point. The lake is the subject of many myths and legends. It is said to contain a large serpent, which is said to have a huge jewel embedded in its head, while other stories tell of a mermaid who sits on the rocks and lures the unsuspecting to a watery death. There are picnic sites around the lake and interpretive signs. A number of other hiking trails start from around the lake. From here it is about 3½ hours walk to Boiling Lake and nearly 2 hours to Grand Fond. There is a short steep climb from Freshwater Lake south-east to a viewpoint overlooking the village of Grand Fond and the Atlantic coast beyond.

It is another three ¾ hour from Freshwater Lake along the trail through elfin woodlands and past several hot and cold springs to the freshwater **Boeri Lake**, formed in the crater of an extinct volcano 2,800ft (854m) above sea level, and covering 4½ acres (2 hectares). As you walk in, there are good views of Morne Trois Pitons,

Dominica's second highest mountain, directly ahead. As you approach the lake, the vegetation changes markedly from tropical rainforest to montane and stunted or elfin growth. Be careful when walking near the water's edge as the stones are very smooth and slippery.

The **Middleham Trails** lead to the tumbling 300ft (91m) **Middleham Falls** and **Tou Santi**, the stinking hole, and can be reached from either Providence on the Laudat road, or the village of Cochrane, just off the Transinsular Road, accessed via Canefield and then taking the inland feeder road, and from Sylvania, where the trail runs through a former coffee plantation now reclaimed by the forest although some of the old buildings can still be seen. The path is easy to follow and clear with steps made from felled trees to help over the steeper sections. Some streams have to be crossed or jumped. The falls plunge for about 200ft (30m) and then tumble in a series of cascades and pools for a futher 100ft (30m). The falls combine with nearby streams to form the Boeri River. The stinking hole is a lava tube which emits sulphur gas. From Providence it is about 1 hour to the falls, but allow almost double from Cochrane. The Cochrane route also provides access to other trails in the northern half of the Morne Trois Pitons National Park.

There is a hiking trail from Laudat which takes you almost to the summit of **Morne Trois Pitons**, named because of its three peaks, the tallest of which is 4,550ft (1,387m).

The **Valley of Desolation** is worth visiting because of its totally volcanic landscape which is unlike anything else on Dominica. The Valley of Desolation gets its name because virtually nothing can grow in the sulphur laden atmosphere. It lies to the side of Morne Watt and is an area of giant rocks, hot springs and bubbling multi-coloured mud pools, with the smell of sulphur obvious long before you reach the valley. There are more than fifty vents in the valley, and the water and rocks in the valley streams are multi-coloured because of the volume of different minerals washed into them from the volcanic soil. It is a 5 mile (8km) hike along a trail from

the village of Laudat. The last volcanic activity was in 1880 when Roseau was covered in a dusting of volcanic ash.

The hike in to the valley and Boiling Lake is quite strenuous up and down hills, down into Breakfast River Valley and then up and over Shark's Tooth Peak at 3,002ft (915m), the highest point on the trail. You should allow at least 4 hours each way.

Titou Gorge is at the beginning of the walk into the Valley of Desolation, and getting to it is not a hike really, more of a swim, as you make your way through the various large rock pools along the floor of the 50ft (15m) high gorge where hot and cold streams meet. The gorge was carved by lava not water.

The trail starts from Laudat, but it is well worth the effort. The trail then passes through lush forest as you climb the slopes of Morne Nicholls, which has stands of Wezinye Montayn, the island's only native conifer.

Boiling Lake, up to 200ft (61m) across, is the second largest of its kind in the world, and gets its name from the gases bubbling up through a fumarole, a flooded vent in the crater in which it has

Following pages: The hot springs and river, Trafalgar Falls

formed. The flow of gases is so powerful that the water level can be raised up to 3ft (1m) because of the bubbling, and steam rising from the water is super heated. Occasionally the gases stop and the water disappears as if going down a giant plug hole, suddenly to re-emerge geyser-like and then the lake fills up again. Be careful to stay on the trail as the earth's crust is very thin in places and if you step off the path you may break through the crust and fall into boiling mud. The nearby **Morne Nicholls** (2,965ft/904m) and **Morne Watt** (4,017ft/1,225m) are named after the two men who in March 1875, made their way to the Boiling Lake and then

subsequently wrote about their exploits in histrionic terms.

The right hand fork at Fond Cani then splits with the left fork providing an alternative access to the Wotten Waven Sulphur Springs, and the right hand fork leading to Morne Prosper.

From the village of **Giraudel** just over 2 miles (3km) inland from Roseau, there is a trail close to the summit of Morne Anglai at 3,683ft (1,123m). The trail, which will take 2 hours to ascend, starts by crossing gardens and ends through elfin woodland. The last leg can be very difficult because of landslides, and caution is advised.

THE WESTERN COAST

As you drive north from Roseau along the coast to Portsmouth, you can appreciate just how difficult it must have been to build the road which connects Dominica's two main towns. In many places the road has had to be carved out of the mountainsides which slope steeply down into the sea. Even well into the twentieth century if you wanted to reach Portsmouth from the capital the only choices

were to take a boat or a circuitous land route through the mountains to the east coast and then travel north to Thibaud before heading inland again to cross the narrowest part of the island to reach Portsmouth.

Today the road still hugs the coastline for most of the way, with the sea on one side and the mountains towering above you on the other.

The road out of Roseau passes

Woodbridge Bay with the cruiser terminal and deep water facility and heads for **Canefield** where you can visit the **Old Mill Cultural Centre** which is open daily. Situated in the grounds of an old plantation you can see the watercourse and water wheel which was used to drive the sugar cane pressing machinery, as well as more modern equipment used on the plantation. The sugar cane fields that used to spread outwards from the centre now house the airport and the industrial estate. The centre also has a fascinating little museum which traces the history of the island back to before the time of Columbus, and has many artifacts depicting Carib life, customs and traditions. You can also see the original mace which was used in the House of Assembly for more than 200 years until replaced by the new in 1978 at the time of Independence. There is also a gallery in the Old Mill displaying the work of local artists and sculptors, including the noted Earle Etienne, Arnold Toulon, Kelvin 'Kelo' Royer and Darius David, regarded as the Father of Dominica's art. There is a woodcarving school in the grounds.

The road then passes **Cane-field Airport**, which has been upgraded with an extended runway, and arrives at **Massacre**, named after an incident in 1674. Governor Warner of St. Kitts had one son by a Carib woman, and another Philip by his English wife. When the Governor died, Carib Warner no longer had anyone to protect him, so he fled to Dominica and became a powerful Carib Chief. In 1674, Philip was chosen by the Governor of the Leeward Islands to lead a military force to Dominica to quell the Caribs. According to legend, the two half-brothers met for a feast, but Philip treacherously stabbed his brother to death and that signalled his troops to start killing the other Caribs. To the right of the road there is a pretty Catholic chapel perched on the hill looking out over the village and the sea beyond.

The road continues through the small fishing village of **Mahaut**, and through **Belfast** where the Dominica Coconut Products' factory is based. This factory recently acquired by a US consortium, has been one of the island's many success stories, turning copra into oil for soaps, cosmetics and detergents. It processes the island's entire crop

Following page: The Old Mill Cultural Centre. This was used as a sugar mill and later for crushing limes for limejuice. It is now used for exhibitions, concerts etc.

Massacre village (above)
Dominica Coconut Products factory at Belfast. Imperial Leather and Palmolive soaps
are made here (below)

and produces such international brands as Imperial Leather and Palmolive for the Caribbean. Belfast is also home of the D-Special Rum Distillery.

The road continues northwards past the large rock outcrop known as **Rodney's Rock**, named after the British Admiral, and up the coast under the shadow of Morne Diablotin. One story suggests the mountain was named after the large black necked petrol, known locally as the diablotin, which nested on the slopes. The bird nested on the ground so it was easy to catch, and its nests easy to raid for eggs, and by the nineteenth century it had disappeared from the island.

As you drive along this stretch between Mahaut and Layou, it is worth slowing down and keeping your eyes on the coconut groves to your left between the beach and the road. At times you can see hundreds of land crabs burrowing in the sand, and the area has so many crabs that it is known locally as 'Crab City'.

Layou is a small fishing village with a pretty black sand beach.

Layou River is the longest on Dominica, and has some beautiful pools just inland from the estuary, and it is a great spot for fishing. There are also longer walks up the Layou River Valley as far as Bells on

the Transinsular route where you can arrange to be picked up. The Layou River Hotel has a wonderful location with the river flowing through its lush and well-tended tropical gardens with towering cliffs behind. It has an excellent restaurant and makes a great place to stay or pop in for a meal.

The land north of the Layou River bridge is the **Hillsborough Estate**, once famous for tobacco production and now growing coconuts, coffee and cocoa. The remains of the old factory can be seen and the estate house still looks out over the valley.

The Castaways Hotel is on Mero Beach beyond the village of **Saint Joseph**. The road then runs close to the Macoucherie Distillery, and then through the small coastal villages of Salisbury, Coulibistri, Colihaut and Dublanc, where there is a feed road providing access inland to Morne Diablotins and the Northern Forest Reserve area and many walks.

A SIDE TRIP TO MORNE DIABLOTINS

The **Northern Forest Reserve** includes Morne Diablotins 4,747ft (1,447m), with the Syndicate area just to the north-west, which is important as the home of the endangered Sisserou and Jaco parrots.

Morne Diablotins, the second highest peak in the Lesser Antilles, was an active volcano millions of years ago, and its frequent eruptions spawned the many other peaks in the north of the island. If you have the chance to view Morne Diablotins (which means Little Devil) from the sea, you can see how all the ridges and valleys fan out from the mountain.

The steep slopes are covered in dense forest but there is a trail to the summit, although you need to allow between 2 or 3 hours, depending on your fitness and stamina, to reach the top. The trail starts from the Syndicate Estate and is reached from a feeder road inland from the main road just north of the fishing village of Dublanc on the west coast.

The feeder road climbs first through dry scrubland and then deciduous woodland up to about 1,700ft (518m) where the trail starts and the tropical rain forest begins. The path scrambles its way upwards through the trees and around the mountain for about 800ft (244m). The path is clear but twists and turns and is steep. It is lucky there is so much

to see because it gives you the excuse to stop frequently — and catch your breath at the same time. The air is often filled with bird calls. You may hear the raucous calls of the Sisserou and Jaco parrot, and you will almost certainly here the songs of the Mountain Whistler, officially known as the Rufous-throated Solitaire. The whistling has been likened by some to the sound of a squeaking gate, but this is very unfair and it is a very melodic, plaintive call.

Here the trees tower 100ft (30m) and more above your heads, while dwarfed by them are beautiful spreading tree ferns with their delicate fronds. If you look down rather than up, you will be rewarded by the sight of insects scurrying around the ground, several species of fungi, and, if it has been raining, you can try and identifying the footprints of animals left in the mud. There are wild pigs in the forest but they tend to stay in the thickest parts of the forest, especially if there are people about, but if it is has been raining, you might be able to see where they have enjoyed a mud bath.

The trees become shorter as you enter the montane forest.

Following pages: Layou River estuary and, (inset) Morne Diablotins

Here the trees are also thinner and this type of forest is appropriately called 'cloud forest'. It is often shrouded in clouds, and as a result, it is wetter and cooler than lower altitudes, and it often seems that a mist hangs between the trees.

The path can be decidely wet underfoot with lots of moss and ferns growing on the swampy ground. The vegetation then changes again, this time to elfin woodland, although it is still part of the cloud forest.This is the steepest part of the trail and you often have to grab branches to help haul yourself over the rock strewn ground.

The final stretch is up over rocky exposed ground covered with lichens and mosses, and then you are on the summit, and if the clouds are not too low, you have magnificient panoramic views. After all the effort of the ascent, you are usually ready for a hearty picnic, and as you eat, scan the surrounding countryside and try to identify all the landmarks spread out around you.

To the south are the mountains: Mornes Trois Pitons, Watt, Ablais and Plat Bays, to the north Morne aux Diables, Morne Espagnol and the Cabrits. To the north and out to sea you can spot Marie Galante, Les Saintes and Guadeloupe, and

if the weather is really clear, some days you can even see Martinique to the south.

The maroons, the slaves who managed to escape in the eighteenth century, used the mountain as a hide out and they often escaped capture by disappearing into what seemed inpenetrable forest.

Dr John Imray and two friends are credited with the first ascent of the mountain in 1868. Accompanied by nine porters and locals armed with machetes to clear a path, they took 2 days and 2 nights to reach the summit, camping out along the way. Today the return trip can be made in 6 or 7 hours but allow extra for your picnic and frequent rest stops. It is a good idea to take a guide if you are not very good at navigating in this sort of terrain. Although the path is easy to follow, some people have taken a wrong turn and been lost in the forest for days.

The **Syndicate Nature Trail** is one of the shortest trails developed by the Forestry Division and one of the most delightful. Although the trail is 1,800ft (549m) above sea level at the foot of Morne Diablotins, the walking is not difficult. The trail is through a 240 acre (96 hectare) section of the forest bought by the Dominican Government in 1989 from private owners with the assistance of RARE Center and the International Council for Bird Preservation, now BirdLife International. Many Dominicans also helped finance the purchase of the land because of its importance. The area is popularly known as the 'parrot preserve' and before it was acquired by the government, logging had started which threatened one of the few remaining habitats of these endangered parrots. The trail was opened in 1994 and runs for four fifths of a mile through superb mature tropical rain forest. A section of the path follows part of the boundary of the 22,000 acre (8,800 hectare) Northern Forest Reserve, and the whole route can be walked in around 30 minutes, although there is so much to see along the way, that it can take very much longer. There are two bridges along the trail crossing streams, but these are usually dry unless there has been a lot of rain.

The walk, although short, offers the chance to spot most of the main tree species found in the island's rain forests, and many of the finest specimens are labelled. There is the giant Gommier, which produces gum and is Dominica's most common species. Its towering trunk is topped by a canopy of leaves which provide food and shelter for a wide range of wildlife. You can spot the speckled barked Bois Diable, which is burnt to produce charcoal, and the Maho Cochon, whose timber is the preferred wood for coffins. There is also the Mang Blanc with its huge supporting roots, and Carapite, which is widely used for heavy construction because it is one of the densest woods on the island. There is also a magnificent specimen of a Chataignier with its enormous buttress roots, which can be visited a little way off the main path.

Most of the trees play host to huge air plants, which would cost a fortune if on sale abroad as the tiniest pieces seem to sell for a few pounds. There are also orchids, Zel-Mouch with its palm-like, leaves and bromeliads, members of the pineapple family, as well as huge 'bird's nest' anthurium. There are three look out points just off the trail, all of which offer views of the Picard River Gorge, and slightly more open vistas of the rain forest. The

Following pages: Portsmouth, where boat trips exploring the Indian River are popular

look-out points also provide the best chances of spotting Dominica's two indigenous species of parrot.

The Sisserou parrot (*Amazona imperialis*) is Dominica's national birds, and one of the rarest of all the Amazon parrot species. The smaller Jaco or red necked parrot (*Amazona arausica*) is more colourful and more plentiful, and both can often be heard calling if not seen.

The blue headed hummingbird, also only found on Dominica, can sometimes be seen along the path, as well as red necked pigeons and broad winged hawks swooping low over the trees. The Mountain Whistler is a beautiful song bird whose calls can frequently be heard. There are no large mammals on the island but large rodents called agoutis frequent the forest, and lizards are plentiful, although often so well camouflaged that you only see them if they move.

There are plans to absorb the Syndicate Nature Trail and the 'parrot preserve' into a much larger National Park covering all the area around Morne Diablotins, and funding for this has now been agreed. This would have the effects of protecting other species of wildlife, as well as the parrots, and safeguarding the headwaters of a number of rivers which supply

drinking water for a number of communities in the north-western part of the island, including the Cabrits Cruise Ship Berth.

Return to the coast and head north through Windward Estates and Glanvillia, to the Indian River.

A SIDE TRIP UP THE INDIAN RIVER

A trip up the Indian River is an experience you are not likely to forget. If possible take a row boat rather than a boat powered with an outboard motor, because the engine will frighten off a lot of the wildlife. You can negotiate a price for the trip with the boat owners either around the jetty in Portsmouth, or by the bridge at the mouth of the estuary just to the south of the town. Expect to pay around EC$15 to 20 a person depending on the number of passengers per boat, and do not forget your camera.

The river is named after the Carib Indians who used to live along its banks. They used the river to get from the village inland to the sea where they fished. Ships anchored for revictualling in Prince Rupert Bay would also send crews in rowing boats up river to trade with the Caribs.

Shortly after setting off up river, you pass the large barges that are towed by tugs and take the bananas out to the ships anchored in the bay. When the banana boat is in, all the small boats lend a hand getting the crop moved as quickly as possible.

You then make a right turn into the 58 acres (23 hectares) of swamp that run aongside the river. The waters here have mullet, pike and crayfish and lots and lots of crabs, especially the small red leg crabs, and larger swamp crabs, Dominica's largest species of land crab. The vegetation is also home to many birds, and you can spot several species of waterfowl and herons, as well as kingfishers, egrets, red necked pigeons and hummingbirds. You might also see an iguana resting in a tree.

The guides-cum boatmen take a great pride in their work and they are very knowledgeable, normally providing a non-stop commentary about the history of the river, area and its wildlife. Their eyes are so sharp they can spot skulking birds, fish and crabs which you would never see without them being pointed out.

The journey gently meanders for about ½ mile (1km) up the river which is lined with mangroves. There are occasional views inland of Morne Espagnol, Morne Destinee and Morne Aux Diables, before the trees meet to form a canopy blocking out the views. The giant Bwa Mang trees have complex root systems, like buttresses on a castle wall, and among the roots edible crabs can be found, although catching them is an art.

Our guide edged towards the roots and then suddenly leapt onto one root, plunging his hand down into the mud, and emerged with a decent sized crab, the meat of which is considered a delicacy. This crab was lucky and was returned to its home. The guide will also point out the many flowers that can be seen along the river banks such as the yellow flowered Mahoe doux, a relative of the Hibiscus family, the giant swamp fern, 'Elephant ears' anthurium, and many orchids.

The water is more than 10ft (3m) deep in places and usually very clear although it does get cloudy after rain. A short way up the river you pass the wrecked railway bridge destroyed by Hurricane David. The railway, the only one built on Dominica, was constructed early in the twentieth century and ran for a short stretch down the west coast. The up journey ends as

Following pages: The coast north of Coulibistri

the river narrows and future progress is blocked by a series of mini rapids. There is, however, a stop over at the ramshackle river bar on the bank among the trees, which serves a variety of rums and local drinks including powerful coconut punches.

If you have time, you can take a short hike inland before making the return journey down the river. The walk crosses small fields of banana, its big brother plantain, and pumpkins, and then across a grass area before plunging back into a forest of freshwater swamp. The walk ends at at the edge of a large marsh which is a favourite resting ground during the winter months for migrating birds.

Before the guided tours up the river started, passing yachts anchored in the bay and used their dinghies to travel up the river. They were light enough to drag across the shallow rapids that block progress for the larger vessels used today, and the river then widens into a series of large pools, before more rapids which again could be waded with care, towing the dinghy behind. Passage up river was finally blocked by a waterfall. While one can still take dinghies up river, it makes sense to let someone else row you up, especially as the boatmen take a pride in their work

and make excellent tour guides.

It is also a good idea to wear light weight clothes, and not many of them. The weather may be perfect when you start your journey up river but within minutes the heavens may open with a tropical downpour. Luckily, it usually does not rain for very long, and the sun soon dries you off.

A trip up the Indian River is a must, not just because it is a delightfully, relaxing ride, but because it does allow you to see a mangrove river and swamp, and all its wildlife, at close hand.

Portsmouth is Dominica's second largest town and was originally planned to be the capital because of its natural harbour in Rodney Bay. The nearby marshes, however, were infested by malaria carrying mosquitoes, and so the settlers decided to relocate the main city in Roseau.

The town has immigration and customs facilities at the police station in Bay Street. These facilities are necessary because Rodney Bay is a very popular anchorage for visiting yachts, and the new specially built cruise dock on the northern side of the bay close to the entrance to the National Park, attracts a growing number of cruise ships. The Cruise Ship Berth and Visitor Centre stands at the foot of Fort Shirley and was opened in 1990 on the site of the old military jetty and dockyard. It is open daily and the hours are extended when a cruise ship is docked. It is the only cruise ship port in the Caribbean where passengers can disembark straight into a National Park.

When a cruise ship is in port, its passengers stream ashore to stroll round the town, swim on the beach, visit the National Park and take a boat trip along Indian River. The bay is also a centre for many trading ships that ply between the Caribbean islands. Within a short distance of the jetty there is a bank, fuel station and tourist information office. There is a cinema and statue of Lord Cathcart.

The market is close to the sea in Bay Street and sells locally produced fruit and vegetables, and inland from it is the Roman Catholic church, and continuing uphill, the small Portsmouth Hospital.

The palm tree lined **Purple Turtle Beach** is one of the finest on the island, and very popular with visitors and islanders living in Roseau. You can buy bread and cakes, drinks and other groceries at the local stores in town.

Portsmouth makes a great place for a very leisurely holiday. You can laze on the beach, take a boat trip down the Indian River, or hire a fishing boat to go out to sea, and there is lots of good walking in the area, both along the coast and inland. The accommodation is mostly in small guest houses, and the local bars and restaurants offer snacks and local specialities.

The best sandy beaches are just to the north of town around the Purple Turtle Beach Club, and this is also the nearest refreshment stop for visitors to the National Park.

EATING OUT IN AND AROUND PORTSMOUTH

Inexpensive	$
Moderate	$$
Expensive	$$$

The Cabin Restaurant $-$$
☎ 445-5695. Snacks and local dishes.

Coconut Beach Restaurant $$-$$$
☎ 445-5393. A near perfect place to enjoy dinner beside the Caribbean. Good food, especially local Creole dishes, friendly service and a great atmosphere.

Douglas Snackette and Restaurant $-$$

THE BATTLE OF THE SAINTS

The Battle of the Saints got its name because it was fought off the Isles des Saintes, between Guadeloupe and Dominica. The French fleet in Fort Royal, Martinique, planned to connect with the Spanish fleet at Cap Francois in Haiti, and then launch an attack on Fort Charles in Jamaica, then commanded by Admiral Horatio Nelson. If successful, the combined French and Spanish attack could well have driven the English out of the Caribbean.

Admiral Rodney's reinforced fleet in 1782 numbered 36 ships of the line, and more than 70 armed support vessels, were anchored off Pigeon Island in St. Lucia. Look-outs on Pigeon Island were able to monitor the French build up at Fort Royal, and on 8 April Rodney received a signal that the French fleet of more than 150 ships and an army of 10,000 men, had set sail. Within 2 hours, the English fleet was also under way and in pursuit.

The French were anxious to avoid a confrontation until they could link up with the Spanish fleet, but Rodney knew he would be outnumbered if this happened. For 3 days, the French fleet eluded the English, but their ships slowed down on the evening of 11 April because of the calmer winds in the lee of Dominica, and overnight Admiral Hood's squadron attacked disabling two of the French ships as the fleets commanded by Rodney and Drake closed in. The first English barrage wreaked havoc, and although the battle raged all day, Admiral de Grasse on his flagship *Ville de Paris*, struck his colours in surrender just before sunset.

☎ 445-5253. Good value snacks, juices and local dishes.

La Flambeau $$-$$$
Picard Beach Cottage Resort
☎ 445-5131. The restaurant overlooks the sea and offers fine

dining with local Creole and International cuisine.

Mango Bar & Restaurant $-$$
☎ 445-3099. Open daily for breakfast and lunch, and Sunday to Thursday for dinner. Try a

Facing page: Fort Shirley

traditional Creole breakfast, and speciality dishes like baked chicken, fish, lobster and sea eggs.

Purple Turtle Beach Club $-$$
☎ 445-5296. Snacks and local dishes, especially fish.

Sango's Sea Lodge $-$$
Picard Estate, Portsmouth
☎ 445-5211. Local Creole dishes and specialising in fish.

A SIDE TRIP TO
CABRITS NATIONAL PARK

The park covers 1,313 acres (525 hectares), including 1,053 acres (421 hectares) of marine area, and there is an enormous amount to see and do, so visits should not be rushed. The site contains the ruins of the eighteenth-century Fort Shirley, the volcanic peaks of East and West Cabrit, tropical forest, the largest swamp on the island, sandy beaches, and coral reefs just offshore to the north.

CABRITS NATIONAL PARK
FORT SHIRLEY

KEY

1 Fort Shirley
2 Officers Quarters
3 Main Guard House
4 Hospital
5 Engineers Quarters/Yard
6 Troops Barracks
7 Hospital
8 Parade Ground

9 Troops Barracks
10 Battery
11 Centre Battery
12 Battery
13 Commandant's House
14 Entrance
15 Cruise Ship Berth

Illustration: Mick Usher

*Cabrits National Park, the duty free shop (above)
and Prince Rupert's Tavern (below)*

You can easily spend a morning visiting the different historic sites and fortifications, and then spend the afternoon, after a picnic lunch, exploring the different habitats and their rich wildlife. Wear sensible footwear as if you want to explore the park thoroughly there are some reasonably steep walks, and after rain, the ground may be slippery. Do not forget your swimming costume so that you can take a cooling off swim in the sea.

If you are planning to spend all day in the park bring plenty of drink and food for lunch, and do not forget camera, binoculars and, if you are a diver, your scuba gear, so you can explore the coral reefs in Douglas Bay.

Prince Rupert Bluff Point marks the western tip of the Cabrits headland which is ideally suited as a fort location. The approaches from land are protected by swamps, and it has commanding sea views from its other three flanks, with the western approaches guarded by steep cliffs which form the bluff, and the surrounding coral reefs a hazard for approaching vessels. The headland is formed by the twin peaks of extinct volcanoes,

East Cabrit 458ft (140m), and **West Cabrit** 560ft (171m) respectively, whose tree covered slopes run down to the sea. From the summits one can look north beyond Douglas Bay to the French islands of Guadeloupe and Les Saintes across the Guadeloupe Channel. To the south there are great views over Prince Rupert Bay, while inland the scenery is dominated by the towering peak of Morne Diablotins, the island's tallest peak.

The park is part of Dominica's National Parks System, and its establishment was made possible by funding from a number of sources in cooperation with the Eastern Caribbean Natural Area Management Programme of the Caribbean Conservation Association. The fort's restoration was supervised by Lennox Honeychurch, who has written many fascinating books about the island's history. The National Park is named after the Portuguese word *cabrit*, which means goat. It was quite common for sailors to leave goats to run wild at various places along routes sailed frequently, so that there would be a constant supply of fresh meat.

The first visitors to Rodney Bay,

Preceding page: Fort Shirley

nowadays Prince Rupert Bay were Amerindians who arrived in their dug out canoes from South America, and after Columbus's 'discovery' of Dominica in 1493 the sheltered waters in the lee of the headland were often used by passing ships. Crews came ashore for water and to trade with the Caribs for food after their Atlantic crossing, and Rodney Bay was particularly popular as an anchorage for Dutch trading ships and Spanish treasure ships. Because of the rich pickings to be had from these Spanish vessels, the waters were also patrolled by English privateers such as Drake, Hawkins, John White and Richard Grenville, as well as French corsairs.

Admiral Horatio Nelson often anchored in these waters as a young officer when serving in the Caribbean fleet, and Prince Rupert of the Rhine landed here in 1652 and explored the hinterland, and subsequently the bay was named after him. It is reported that Stephen Decatur, one of the United States Navy's most colourful characters, fought a duel on the beach. While there is no record of this, Decatur did die as a result of wounds received fighting a duel in Maryland in 1820.

For more than 50 years whalers from Massachusetts used Rodney Bay as their base, Ann Davison, the British yachtswoman, became the first woman to sail the Atlantic single handed, when she landed in Rodney Bay in 1953 after her 65 day voyage in 23ft (7m) *Felicity Ann*. Today, the bay is just as popular with mariners, and attracts yachts from around the world.

The suggested way of visiting the park is to visit Fort Shirley, the valley and Commandant's House, the Centre Battery at the top of the Inner Cabrit, then back down to the Douglas Bay Battery, and finally, the fortifications and buildings that make up the Outer Cabrit perched on Prince Rupert Bluff. When exploring take pictures but nothing else, and leave nothing behind but footprints.

After the Treaty of Paris ceded Dominica to Britain in 1763, engineers and surveyors were quickly dispatched to the island to draw up plans for towns, plantations and coastal defences. From 1771 a small military force was stationed on Cabrits because of its obvious strategic importance, and Royal Engineers started work on **Fort Shirley** in the hollow between the two volcanic domes. The fort was designed by Royal Engineer lieutenant Charles Shipley, but overall control was in the hands of General Thomas Shirley, later Governor of

Dominica, and it was named after him. Building continued on and off until 1826. In the early nineteenth century the fort was one of the most formidable military installations in the West Indies. During its history more than 50 different military buildings were constructed on the garrison grounds and 33 cannon guarded the sea approaches. Because of the frequent changes of occupation, the fort was started by the British to protect ships of the Royal Navy which used Prince Rubert Bay, but added to by the French between 1778 and 1783 when they were in control. At its height the fort consisted of the main fortified garrison, seven gun batteries, seven huge cisterns for gathering and storing drinking water, powder magazines, ordnance stores, barracks and officers' quarters to house the 5 to 600 men stationed there, and room for another 500 men in the event of an emergency, as well as the Commandant's House. Volcanic stone was used to construct the massive ramparts.

The fort saw action on several occasions, particularly during the American War of Independence when the French allied with America against Britain, during the French Revolution when unrest spread throughout the islands, and during the Napoleonic Wars. The biggest and most decisive naval battle ever fought in the Caribbean, the Battle of the Saints, took place within sight of the ramparts of Fort Shirley.

Fort Shirley was also the scene of the revolt of the 8th West India Regiment. The regiment was made up of Afro-West Indian soldiers with British officers. The men mutinied against the appalling conditions they had to live in, they seized the fort in April 1802 and controlled it for 3 days until persuaded to surrender.

The fort was finally abandoned in 1854 and quickly fell into disrepair. Many of the buildings were damaged as stone was removed for construction in Portsmouth and elsewhere, and the ruins quickly became overgrown as the forest once more took over. Some cannon were removed, but many more were left where they were, and attempts are now under way to restore them. Work began on stabilising buildings and the ramparts in 1982, and the small **Fort Shirley Museum**, open daily 10am-5pm (hours may vary), has been established featuring both the parks history and natural history. Other buildings have been turned into an educational and visitors centre.

Today you can literally follow in

The east coast, south of Melville Hall Airport

the footsteps of the soldiers of almost 200 years ago. The paths that lead to the fort from the entrance, to the Inner and Outer Cabrit areas and to the Douglas Bay battery, are all the ones that the military used originally.

The grounds are also the home to a wealth of wildlife and you can spot quite large lizards and iguanas. The freshwater swamps which protect the entrance to the reserve are a bird watcher's dream, especially during the migration season, when they are the temporary home to scores of birds on passage. A study in 1985 conducted by local schoolchildren and the state Forestry and Wildlife Division identified ninety-two tree and plant species in the park, almost all of which had medicinal, edible or other practical uses, such as bathing aids and craftwork applications.

The coral reefs in **Douglas Bay** are also protected as part of the National Park, and the palm and almond tree fringed beach along the bay makes a great place for a picnic. There is a fascinating underwater trail for snorkellers, which is marked out by white buoys in the middle of the bay. The coral grows on top of volcanic rock outcrops, and the bay floor is covered with sea grass, home to shoals of brightly coloured tropical fish. For more adventurous divers, there are rock and coral formations to be explored at the foot of the cliffs at the northern end of the bay. Local fishing can be hired for the short trip to the cliffs, or for trips further afield.

From Portsmouth the road runs north to Douglas Bay and Toucari Bay just beyond. Estates along the coast here were awakened to the sound of cannon fire on the morning of 12 April 1782 and had a grandstand view of the Battle of the Saints fought offshore. The

road then runs north through Morne Soleil, Cottage and Clifton to Capucin and the Capucin Cape on the north-east tip of the island. The waters off the coast can be very rough and there are a number of shipwrecks off the cape. You have to return to Portsmouth along the same road.

Just north of Portsmouth there is a feeder road which runs up into the foothills around Morne aux Diables, and from here you can visit the Tanatane Waterfall and the mountain.

The main road from Portsmouth cuts inland through palm forests for about 6 miles (10km) — through what is known as 'coconut country' — to the north-eastern coast and some of the island's finest beaches.

THE EAST COAST

The road that crosses the island and is now used to travel between Roseau and Melville Hall Airport was started in 1909 and at the time, had the grand name of the Imperial Road. It finally emerged on the east coast in 1956, by which time it had been re-named the Transinsular Road.

From Roseau, you reach it by

driving north to Canefield where it strikes inland from the coast road. The drive is a spectacular one with magnificent tropical rain forest on either sides of the road as you climb up into the mountains and then descend down to the eastern coast. It is not a fast road and there are quite a lot of sharp bends, but motorists use their horns a lot to warn each other of their approach round blind corners. In the mountains if it is not raining, then it will be soon! Rain starts as quickly as it ends but it can make the roads slippery and after very heavy downpours, mud and other debris may be washed on to the road.

The Middleham Trails lead south from the road into the Roseau Valley to the impressive Middleham Falls and then on to the village of Laudat. If you want to do this walk, it is a good idea to have a taxi waiting for you at the other end, and take a guide.

The road runs through Roger and Pont Cassé where there is a police post. Morne Trois Pitons is only 2 miles (3km) or so to the south-east but often difficult to spot because of the dense vegetation.

At Point Cassé the road splits into three, the left fork curves back into the Layou Valley and runs on to the west coast, the middle fork (the main road) runs through the Central Forest Reserve and Carib Territory to the east coast at Pagua Bay, and the right fork runs roughly parallel to this, hitting the east coast just south of Castle Bruce near Anse Quanery. If you want to explore the east coast between La Plaine and Delices you must take this road, as it is not possible to drive all the way south from Castle Bruce.

VISITING EMERALD POOL & THE EAST COAST BETWEEN ROSALIE & DELICES

You take the right hand Castle Bruce fork to visit **Emerald Pool**, a grotto with its own mini waterfall and small pool, surrounded by lush vegetation and tropical plants, flowers and ferns. The pool, which is in the northern part of the Morne Trois Piton National Park, is a gentle 10 minute walk through woodland from the road, about 3 miles (5km) north-east from Pont Cassé. The looped trail is through rich vegetation with Gommier trees and the Mang Blanc with its huge buttress roots. The thick canopy discourages too many ground plants but epiphytes flourish and some giant ones can be seen around the pool, together with huge ferns, orchids and anthuriums. There is a short section of trail paved with slabs of rock laid by the Caribs and used by them as a main route. This area is rich in birdlife, especially for hummingbirds and the elusive Mountain Warbler. Jaco parrots can also sometimes be seen around the pool.

The Emerald Bush Bar and Restaurant at Emerald Pool is about the only place to eat in the area. The bar, overlooking L'Or River, offers quick snacks, while

THE MAROONS

The Maroons were escaped slaves who evaded capture by living in settlements deep in the forest. Their history is a fascinating one, and no one is sure when the first slaves escaped to Dominica. It is known, however, that some unfortunates who managed to escape from neighbouring islands and made it to Dominica thinking they were safe, were captured and enslaved by the Caribs. It is even thought that the Caribs may have launched attacks on other islands in order to capture slaves to work their fields.

When the first French settlers arrived at the beginning of the eighteenth century, there were already some Maroons living in forest settlements. They were called Les Negres Marron by the French, and in the confusion that accompanied the British takeover of the island, many French slaves, particularly from the Grand Bay area, took the opportunity to escape and join the Maroons. Realising what would happen to them if they were caught, the Maroons conducted a campaign of guerilla war against the British, and they proved fearsome adversaries.

The Maroon built their first large settlements in the south of the island and they developed a system of inland trails that allowed them to travel quickly whenever necessary. They were expert at moving through and living off the jungle.

It is only in the last 30 years or so that roads capable of taking motor traffic have been built across the island, and for centuries the only method of travel was on foot through the jungle. As the early French settlers discovered, they were most vulnerable to attack from the Caribs when they entered the forest, and so they learned to stay out. Although there were clashes between the Maroons and the French, for most of the time they did not come into contact with each other.

The Maroons worst clashes, however, occurred after the British had taken over the island in 1783 and these led to the Maroon Wars. By this time, a series of maroon camps has been built in the south and the centre of the island, and each camp was led by a chieftain. The Maroons conducted an underground war skirmishing with the British and then vanishing back into the forests, and at night, sending messengers or 'recruiting agents', into the plantations urging the slaves to escape.

In the south reception camps for escaped slaves were established by the Maroons inland of Grand Bay where there were many plantations. The slaves were then taken to other more remote camps where they were safer. Some of the feeder roads now used to travel inland from Colihaut follow the paths of the original maroon trails. There were more reception camps here established by chieftain Pharcell.

There were thirteen prominent chieftains who led the campaign against the British. Balla, Congo Ray, Gicero, Hall, Juba, Jupiter, and Zombie were the leading chieftains in the south, above Grand Fond on the east coast was the camp of Mabouya, overlooking Colihaut was Pharcell, and near the head of the Layou Valley were the camps of Greg, Gorée, Jacko and Sandy. The guerilla campaign was not just conducted by the men. The camps had women and children, and many of the women became famous for their exploits and fighting skills.

The Maroons became such a problem to the plantation owners that a special tax was levied to fund a militia, but although it was well armed and the men had smart uniforms, it was mostly ineffective against the Maroons.

In 1786 troops from colonial regiments were drafted in to fight alongside the militia, and the situation deteriorated rapidly into the First Maroon War. The soldiers carried out a string of atrocities against the Maroons, and most prisoners were painfully and publicly put to death to deter other slaves from escaping. Hostilities continued over the next 25 years with more slaves escaping to join the Maroons, and more soldiers needed to try to contain them. The Last Maroon War, fought between 1812 and 1814, was a deliberate attempt by the British, led by Governor Ainslie, to wipe out all the remaining Maroons.

Although Emancipation in 1834 gave all the slaves their freedom, it was too late for the Maroons, but the names and valour are not forgotten. The names of many of their camps and chieftains can still be seen as place names on the maps of Dominica. You can visit Morne Negre Maroon, Fond Zombie, Camp Solei, Gorée and Jacko Flats, and you can walk the Grand Fond trail to visit the old water mill at Rosalie, scene of bitter fighting in 1786. Many of the trails in use today were carved out by the Maroons.

Literally carved out are the incredible Jacko Steps, about 1 mile (2km) west of the village of Belles in the Layou Gorge. The steps rise for 300ft (91m) to the site of the chief's camp which was built on a flat plateau surrounded on three sides by sheer cliffs. Jacko was finally tracked down here in 1814 and fatally shot having eluded capture for more than 40 years. The steps cut into the volcanic rock look as if they were built for a giant because of the distance between each of them but this was deliberate. The Maroons could usually take their time scaling the steps, but they were too steep for attackers to rush them. Several attempts by the British to storm the camp failed and it was not overrun until the number of defenders had been greatly reduced by a much larger force of British troops. You can still walk the steps which are kept clear by the schoolchildren in Belles.

the restaurant is noted because of Chef Peter's fine Creole country cuisine. The restaurant and bush hotel are about a ¼ mile (1km) off the main road along a signposted private road.

A short distance beyond the pool, this road forks again near the Tarrish Pit quarry, with the left hand fork going to Castle Bruce, and the right fork (our road) running further south through banana and citrus groves until reaching the coast at **Rosalie** at the mouth of the Rosalie River. You can still see the old aquaduct which used to carry the river water to the sugar mill. There is also the ruins of a church, one of the few traces of the village that once flourished. Ships used to anchor at Rosalie Point to load crops grown on the estates along this part of the coast. From Rosalie there is a feeder road inland to Grand Fond, which follows the old pathway which was actually used to cross the island.

Our road, however, continues south through Riviere Ciriques and Morne Jaune down to **La Plaine**, named by the French because the area inland was reasonably flat compared with the mountainous terrain everywhere else. This area was favoured by the French and many large plantations existed here. Just before entering La

Plaine you pass **Bout Sable Bay**. The black side beach is fringed with palm trees with towering cliffs to the north and heavy surf offshore. It is a delightful place for a picnic and paddle, but not the place for a swim. In 1940 a wealthy American and his wife were saved from drowning here, and in gratitude to the villagers who rescued them, he built La Plaine's first health centre. Their house was the current Springfield Hotel. Inland at the head of the valley is the Sari Sari waterfall.

There is a memorial at Case O'Gowerie to villagers who died during protests against the imposition of a land tax in 1893. They were shot by a force of Marines and police landed at La Plaine from the warship HMS *Mohawk*.

The road then continues south crossing the Boetica Gorge to Delices, La Roche and the Victoria Falls, which can be glimpsed up the valley. The road actually ends close to Pointe Mulatre Bay and the estuary of the White River which runs from the Boiling Lake. The mineral laden waters are reputed to have therapeutic properties so a swim is a good idea, if only to cool down. On the other side of the river there is an old French graveyard and several ruins of the once flourishing sugar and coffee plantation. Although the road ends, walkers can continue south to link up with the road at Petite Savane.

VISITING THE REST OF THE EAST COAST

The main trans-island road runs north from Pont Cassé for a while through the northern part of the Morne Trois Pitons National Park into the Central Forest Reserve. Huge swathes of dasheen deck the mountain sides while vines snake up into the massive trees, and the elegant tree ferns spread their huge fronds out like delicate parasols.

At **Belles** there is a trail, an old Maroon path, which cuts down to the west coast along the Layou Valley. It is about an 8 mile (13km) hike but you can swim part of the way and cool off in the water.

The road then crosses **Carib Territory** to the coast. This area covers 3,700 acres (1,480 hectares) of land with an extensive shoreline and agricultural land behind. The land was given back to the descendants of the island's

original inhabitants in 1903. A hereditary king was appointed chieftain but the title fell into misuse until the 1950s, when a new chief was elected. It continues to be an elected post.

Today the Caribs engage mostly in fishing and agriculture. They still make their traditional dug out canoes by hand using adze, axe and drill and bit. These canoes, assisted by a sail, carried the Caribs throughout the Eastern Caribbean. The canoes are still used for fishing and the Caribs seem to have no problem at all heading out to sea against the prevailing winds and through the Atlantic breakers even in the roughest seas. They normally launch their boats early in the morning, returning with their catch in the afternoon to shoot the surf with the winds behind them to drive the canoes up on to the beach. They also practice their ancient skills of pottery and basket weaving. The weavers are so expert that they can make baskets that are watertight.

Concord and Floral Gardens Hotel are off the main road about 3 miles (5km) inland. The guest house overlooks the Carib Indian Reserve and stands at the foot of the

Following pages: There are several picturesque beaches on the north coast. This one is near Calibishie

tropical rain forest. It has won awards for its 'creative environment', and its Island Restaurant serves local Creole cuisine. There is also a Carib craft shop, and the opportunity for river bathing and hikes. In fact, there are several craft shops on the road south through Carib Territory.

A new 'model' Carib village is being built in the territory. It will feature a typical community hut in which traditional arts and crafts will be carried out.

Once at the coast, you have two options: to head north and explore the eastern coast as far north as Point Jaco on the north-eastern tip of the island, or to head south to explore the coast down to as far as Petit Soufrière where the road runs out.

NORTH ALONG THE COAST FROM PAGUA BAY TO POINT JACO

The road between Pagua Bay and Carib Point on the north-eastern tip of the island offers some of the most spectacular and unspoiled beaches on the island. The first section of the road to Crompton Point takes the brunt of the Atlantic rollers crashing in from the east because it faces them almost head on. This is an area of cliffs with many small coves and beaches but these are not suitable for swimming.

The villages of **Marigot** and **Wesley**, with its high school, both on Londonderry Bay, were founded in the late nineteenth century when a British chocolate company bought up many of the old estates to produce their own cocoa. The islanders did not want to became estate workers again, so labour was recruited from neighbouring English speaking islands, including Antigua. As a result, the people have no French traditions, speak no French Creole and are Methodist, rather than Roman Catholic, which is how Wesley gets its name, after brothers Charles and John Wesley, the founders of Methodism.

Melville Hall, the island's main airport, is between Marigot and Wesley and the main runway runs inland parallel with the Melville River. Although the airport was first suggested in the 1940s it was not until the trans-island road was completed that work could start, and the first flight into Melville Hall landed in 1981. The area around Melville Hall has got to be one of the finest settings of any airport with coconut groves, palm trees and the Atlantic Ocean rolling onto the black sands of Londonderry Beach. Most of the coconut groves around the airport are owned by the Larvell family.

A new international airport, capable of taking large jets, has been earmarked with Woodford Hill just over 3 miles (5km) up the coast as the preferred location. Work is not likely to start, however, for some years.

There is a dramatic change in the coastline once you turn **Crompton Point**. The last bay south of the point is the appropriately named **Rough Bay**, but once you drive round the point, the seas become calm and this stretch of coastline has some fabulous beaches. While the stretch of road from Pagua to the point faces nearly due east, the stretch between Crompton Point and Chuval Blanc Point faces due north and the sandy beaches are largely sheltered from onshore winds by cliffs and headlands.

Pointe Baptiste is one of the most idyllic spots on the island. The main house, a typical West Indian timbered home with shaded balcony, is now a guest house and sits atop the red cliffs with magnificent views out to sea, while guest cottages are dotted around it. Inland there are forests and wildlife to spot, and beneath the cliffs is a secluded beach with both black and white sands. The main house has played host over the years to many famous people

including Noel Coward, Somerset Maugham and Princess Margaret.

Next is **Calibishie**, a charming village with its pretty houses and well kept gardens, and protected palm tree fringed, golden sand beach. There is a 1 mile (2km) long reef just offshore which creates a shallow lagoon which offers safe swimming. After cooling off in the sea, you can enjoy a drink at the Almond Tree Restaurant by the beach in the heart of the village.

Just off Calibishie are two rocks sticking out of the sea close together. They used to be joined in a natural arch, known locally as the Gateway to Hell.

At **Hampstead** you can stop and see the men and women sitting close to the road cracking open the coconuts which are then placed in ovens and baked for about 2 days. The contents are then removed and sent off for pressing at the Dominica Coconut Products factory in Belfast on the west coast, while the shells are used to fire the ovens for the next batch.

As you drive around the coast through mostly coconut estates, you will also spot banana groves and occasionally see red bananas.

The small fishing village of **Anse de Mai** gets its name from a French officer who was in charge of a massacre of the Caribs here in 1635.

From Chuval Blanc Point the coastline then runs north-west. This is an area of steep cliffs with many fast running streams tumbling into the sea down waterfalls. In many places the streams have cut their own gorges as they make their way to the sea and nearby there are small villages perched on top of the windswept cliffs. The road needs to be driven with care because it has many hair pin bends and blind corners, but the views are incredible — but remember to pull off the road safely to enjoy them.

At **Vielle Case** you can visit the stone Catholic church with its red roof, flat topped tower and interesting murals; and make your way down to the beach to watch the fishermen launch their boats through the fierce surf of Autrou Bay. The village of Pennville was settled first by the French, as was Vielle Case, and both still have strong French traditions. The road ends at Pennville but there is a track north to Point Jaco, and a nature trail which cuts across the tip of the island to Capucin. From the village you can also visit the Bwa Nef Waterfalls.

There are plans to build a road through the mountains which will connect Pennville and Douglas Bay, but no start date has been announced.

EATING OUT ON THE EAST COAST

Inexpensive	$
Moderate	$$
Expensive	$$$

The Almond Beach Restaurant & Bar $-$$ Calibishie

☎ 445-7783. This is the only place to eat along the north coast. Good local food in a wonderful setting.

SOUTH ALONG THE COAST TO PETIT SOUFRIÈRE

The Carib village of **Salybia**, sometimes called Salibia, is worth visiting for its church. The altar of the Roman Catholic Church of St. Marie at Salybia is made in the shape of a dug out canoe and is an incredible work of art. Walk down the hill to the mouth of the Crayfish River where the water cascades over the rocks into the sea.

At **Sineku** just south of the village you should visit the L'Escalier Tête Chien, which means 'The Snake's Staircase'. It is

Rich foliage surrounds the Hampstead River. Coconuts at the roadside by the Hampstead River (inset)

a solidified lava flow, like a giant writhing serpent, which runs down the hill side and protrudes out into the sea. It figures prominently in Carib folklore and legends. There are a number of craft shops along this stretch of coast road.

At **Castle Bruce** there is the road inland leading back past the Emerald Pool and connecting with the main trans-island route. The road runs through the Belle Fille Valley and then onto a long straight stretch which runs through the former Castle Bruce sugar cane estate, now split up into a number of small farms.

You can usually see Carib canoes under the palms along Anse Quanary, also known as St. David Bay, and early in the day you may see the men putting out to sea. Because of the strong currents here, however, the sea is not suitable for swimming.

The drive down to Petite Soufrière offers tremendous views both up and down the coast. At **Saint Sauveur** on Grand Marigot Bay, there is a charming little church and a handful of small bay oil distilleries.

The small village of **Petite Soufrière** is the end of the road and something of a mystery, as there is no evidence of any volcanic activity in the area. The houses are built on the steep wind beaten slopes. There is a trail which allows you to continue south on foot towards Rosalie.

Traveller's Tips

Rosalie Diocesan Centre

ARRIVAL, ENTRY REQUIREMENTS & CUSTOMS

An immigration form has to be filled in and presented on arrival. The form requires you to say where you will be staying on the island, and if you plan to move around, put down the first hotel you will be staying at. The immigration form is in two parts, one of which is stamped and returned to you in your passport. You must retain this until departure when the slip is retrieved as you check in at the airport.

British citizens and those from European Community and Commonwealth countries need a valid passport for entry, but a visa is not required. Visas are only required by citizens of foreign countries.

You may also be asked to show that you have a return ticket before being admitted. Visitors from the United States and Canada staying less than 6 months can enter on an I.D. card but must have valid return tickets. French citizens with a Carte Identité are allowed to visit for up to 2 weeks.

If travelling on business, a letter confirming this, may prove helpful in speeding your way through customs, especially if travelling with samples.

Having cleared immigration, you will have to go through customs, and it is quite usual to have to open your luggage for inspection. If you have expensive cameras, jewellery etc it is a good idea to travel with a photocopy of the receipt. The duty free allowance entering Dominica is 200 cigarettes or half a pound of tobacco or 50 cigars, and one quart of spirits or wine.

ACCOMMODATION

Dominica has a wide range of accommodation to suit all tastes and pockets, from top class hotels to delightful guest houses, self-catering apartments and beach cottages. Many of the new hotel developments have been planned with great regard for the environment, and several have won eco-tourism awards for their skilful use of natural materials which blend harmoniously with their unspoiled surroundings.

If you want to eat out and explore quite a lot, it may pay to stay in a hotel offering part board, or one of the guest houses on the island, some of them converted plantation homes, and generally offering excellent value for money.

There are also apartments,

holiday villas and beach cottages available for rent offering you the privacy of your own accommodation and the flexibility to eat in or out.

Some terms: MAP stands for Modified American Plan ie breakfast and dinner are included. EP or European Plan means bed only and no meals. CP is Continental Plan which is bed and breakfast, and AP for American Plan, means room and all meals. Prices quoted by hotels are for rooms, whether one or two people are sharing, and you may find it diffucult to get a reduction if you are travelling alone, but have a go. Prices, unless clearly stated, do not usually include the 8 per cent government tax and 10 per cent service charge. $ represents inexpensive accommodation, $$ moderate, and $$$ de-luxe.

An A-Z of Accommodation
Hotels

Ambassador Hotel $ EP, CP, MAP, Canefield, PO Box 413, Roseau ☎ 449-1501. It is 2 minutes from Canefield Airport, and has 10 rooms, a restaurant, bar and conference facilities.

Anchorage Hotel $-$$ EP,CP, MAP, Castle Comfort, PO Box 34, Roseau ☎ 448-2638. It has 32

rooms, restaurant, bar, pool, squash, conference facilities and special honeymoon packages. It has a full service PADI diving centre on the premises, and its own 41ft (12½m) custom diveboat. Organised excursions including whale watching trips can be arranged.

Casa Ropa Hotel $ EP, Portsmouth ☎ 445-5492. It has 8 rooms and restaurant but self catering facilities are also available.

Castaways Beach Hotel $$ EP, Mero, PO Box 5, Roseau ☎ 449-6244. The island's only beach hotel surrounded by tropical gardens, offering 26 beachfront rooms. Creole and international dishes are served in the terraced Almond Tree Restaurant. Sailing, water skiing and tennis are available, and the hotel is a certified PADI diving centre. Tuition is available as well as night dives and wall dives.

Castle Comfort Lodge $$ MAP, Castle Comfort, PO Box 63, Roseau ☎ 448-2188. It has 10 rooms and restaurant, and offers diving and honeymoon packages.

Coconut Beach Hotel $-$$ CP, MAP, Picard, PO Box 37, Roseau ☎ 445-5393. It has 22 rooms, a bar and restaurant specialising in local Creole cuisine, and offers tours, car rentals, diving and honeymoon packages.

Emerald Bush Hotel $ EP, MAP. Emerald Pool Road ☎ 448-4545. 8 rooms.It has a restaurant and also offers self-catering facilities.

Evergreen Hotel $$ CP, Castle Comfort, PO Box 309, Roseau ☎ 448-3288. It is 1 mile (2km) south of Roseau and has 16 double rooms. It has a restaurant specialising in local cuisine, bar and pool set in tropical gardens. Diving and island day tours can be arranged.

Fort Young Hotel $$-$$$ EP, CP, MAP, Roseau ☎ 448-5000. A luxury but affordable hotel in delightful historic buildings in Roseau, close to the water and the old town. It has 33 well appointed air-conditioned rooms, excellent restaurant, bar, pool, conference facilities, direct dial telephones in the rooms and honeymoon and diving packages.

The Garraway Hotel $$ EP, Bayfront, Roseau ☎ 448-3247. A modern hotel with 32 well appointed rooms on the waterfront and close to all Roseau's amenities. It has 31

rooms, a restaurant, bar, shops, conference facilities and tours and hikes can be arranged.

Lauro Club $$ EP, CP, MAP, Salisbury ☎ 449-6602. It has 16 units with ocean and mountain views, noted restaurant and self catering facilities, pool and diving packages with East Carib Dive.

Layou River Hotel $ EP, CP, MAP, Clarke Hall, Roseau ☎ 449-6081. Nestled on the banks of the Layou River, the hotel makes an ideal base for touring and hiking in the area both along the west coast and inland along the river valley towards Emerald Pool and Carib Territory. It has 35 rooms, award winning terrace restaurant offering local specialities, bar, pool and conference facilities and offers honeymoon packages.

Mamie's On the Beach $ EP, Portsmouth ☎ 445-4295. A delightful small hotel with 8 rooms right on the beach, with charming gardens, and good restaurant. It also offers honeymoon packages.

Papillote Wilderness Retreat $ EP, Trafalgar Falls Road ☎ 448-2287. It has 10 rooms, a restaurant and a self catering cottage by a waterfall.

Picard Beach Cottage Resort $$
EP, Picard ☎ 445-5131. It has 16
rooms, a restaurant and also offers
self catering facilities, pool,
conference facilities, diving and
honeymoon packages.

Portsouth Beach Hotel $ EP,
Picard ☎ 445-5142. It is located
on one of Dominica's finest,
unspoiled golden sand beaches.
It has 96 rooms, a beach
restaurant and bar, pool, and
offers honeymoon packages. It
also has a dive centre and offers a
wide range of watersports, as
well as hiking, tours and
birdwatching. It also has
conference facilities.

Reigate Hall Hotel $$ EP, Reigate
☎ 448-4031. A very attractive
small hotel with 16 rooms and
rustic charm. The unique hanging
restaurant offers International
cuisine as well as Creole
specialities. There is a pool,
sauna, bar, and diving and
honeymoon packages are
available.

Reigate Waterfront Hotel
(formerly Sisserou) $-$$ EP, MAP,
Castle Comfort ☎ 448-3130. It has
24 rooms, restaurant and pool,
and offers diving and honeymoon
packages.

Sutton Place $$ Roseau ☎ 448-
4313. In the heart of Roseau's
business centre, and has five cosy
rooms and three suites with fully
equipped kitchens. The restaurant
offers Creole cuisine and you can
enjoy spectacular sunsets from
the rooftop garden.

Symes-Zee Villa $$ Laudat
☎ 448-3337. This is a new hotel,
set among magnificent forest and
mountain scenery just 15 minutes
from Roseau. It has a restaurant
and bar, and can arrange diving,
hiking and other island tours.

<u>Guest Houses</u>
Bon Marche $ EP.11 Old Street,
Roseau ☎ 448-2083. 4 rooms.

Canefield Overnighter $ EP.
Roseau ☎ 449-1378. 3 rooms.

Carib Territory Guest House $
EP. Crayfish River, Carib Territory,
☎ 445-7256. 8 rooms. The
restaurant is noted for its authentic
Carib and Creole cuisine. There is
great hiking and day tours can be
organised. It is also noted for its
arts, crafts, culture and artifacts.

*Facing page: The Garraway Hotel, Roseau (above)
and the Springfield Plantation Hotel*

Cherry Lodge $ EP. CP. Roseau ☎ 448-2366. 6 rooms.

Continental Inn $ 37 Queen Mary Street, Roseau ☎ 448-7022. 11 rooms. Friendly and cosy in the heart of town, with a bar and Creole restaurant.

Douglas Guest House $ EP. Portsmouth ☎ 445-5253. 9 rooms. It has a restaurant and also offers self-catering facilities.

End of Eden Guest House $ EP. 2 Princess Lane, Goodwill, Roseau Valley ☎ 448-8272. 7 rooms. It offers honeymoon packages.

Floral Gardens $ EP. Concord ☎ 445-7636. 18 rooms. The guest house overlooks the Carib Indian Reserve, is at the foot of the tropical rain forest, and is only a short drive from the beaches. It has won awards for its 'creative environment'. It serves local Creole cuisine at the Island Restaurant, has a Carib craft shop, and also offers river bathing, hikes and tours. There are special packages for honeymooners.

Gachette's Seaside Lodge $ 26 Kennedy Avenue, Scott's Head, Roseau ☎ 448-4551. In the island's main fishing village and across the road from the caribbean's most

beautiful pebble beach. It has 10 rooms, bar and restaurant.

Hummingbird Inn $ EP, CP, MAP. Morne Daniel ☎ 449-1042. It has 10 rooms, self catering facilities surrounded by wonderful scenery. The beach and rivers are a short stroll away. The restaurant offers local and international cuisine. Honeymoon packages are offered.

Kent Anthony Guest House $ EP, CP, MAP. 3 Great Marlborough Street, Roseau. ☎ 448-2730. It has 19 rooms and restaurant.

Layou Valley Inn $-$$ EP, CP, MAP. Layou Valley ☎ 449-6203. Set in the mountains, it has 5 comfortable rooms and a restaurant offering Country French cuisine. Restaurant reservations are recommended. There is also a pool and self catering facilities if required, as well as diving packages.

Rhema Guesthouse, $ 1 Canal Lane/Federation Drive, Goodwill ☎ 448-7170. Formerly the Goodwill Inn, this comfortable and friendly guesthouse is ideal for families, and small business groups.

Roxy's Mountain Lodge $ EP, MAP. Laudat ☎ 448-4845. This 6 bedroom house is at the gateway to the National Park, and has a Creole restaurant and pool. It offers guided tours and honeymoon packages.

St. Theresa's Guest House $ 90 Queen Mary Street, Roseau ☎ 448-4223. In the heart of town in a large traditional home with overhanging balconies.

Springfield Plantation Guest House $-$$ EP, CP, MAP. Springfield ☎ 449-1401. 6 rooms A former plantation house and now a modernised delightful inn although it has retained much of its original furnishings. It has a restaurant, and stands at 1,200ft (366m) above sea level in tropical gardens with superb views. The grounds also house the Archbold Tropical Research Centre, which makes a great base from which to study and explore the island's natural history.

Vena's $ EP. 48 Cork Street, Roseau ☎ 448-3286. It has 17 rooms and restaurant.

Vena's Paradise Resort $ CP. Pond Casse. ☎ 449-2001. It has 5 rooms and restaurant.

Wykie's La Tropical $ EP. 51 Old Street, Roseau ☎ 448-8015. In the heart of town with 6 rooms, restaurant and bar and every day happy hours between 12noon and 2pm and 4-6pm.

Apartments and Cottages

Blanca Heights $ Picard ☎ 445-5288. A 10 minute walk down to the beach and offering excellent views over Portsmouth. Accommodation is in 12 self-catering apartments.

Casaropa Apartments $$ Portsmouth ☎ 445-5492. Self contained apartments with restaurant, bar and laundry.

Castille Apartment $ Scott's Head, ☎ 448-2926. 3 rooms

Chez Ophelia $ Copthall ☎ 448-3438. Ten Dominican-style cottage apartments close to Trafalgar Falls and Wootten Waven hot springs, and minutes from Roseau. It offers honeymoon packages, and tours and hikes can be arranged.

D'Auchamps Apartment $ Trafalgar ☎ 448-3346. 4 rooms. This is a small self contained one bedroom apartment on D'Auchamps Estate in the Roseau Valley close to the National Park and many hiking trails.

Eileen Shillingford Apartment $
15 St. Aroment, Goodwill, Roseau
☎ 448-2986. 3 units

Emerald Carib Cottages $$
Emerald Pool Road ☎ 448-4545. It
has two cottages, a restaurant
noted for its Creole cuisine, a
bush bar overooking the l'Or
River, part of the 24 acre (10
hectare) Emerald Nature Park, and
Carib Cottages and bungalow
rooms among the trees.

Exotica $$ Morne Anglais
☎ 448-7895. Eight Caribbean-style
wooden cottages blend in with
the magnificent scenery on the
tree clad slopes of the mountain.
Self catering facilities are available
and you can also enjoy local
cuisine in the restaurant prepared
from produce grown organically
on nearby farms.

Flamboyant Apartments $ Picard
Bay Street, Portsmouth
☎ 445-4194. Self-contained
beach apartments on Picard
Beach. Tours, snorkelling, scuba,
hiking and boat charters can
be arranged.

Gallion-on-Sea $ Soufrière
☎ 448-2194. One unit.

Hampstead Country House $$
Hampstead ☎ 445-5253. One unit
It has a restaurant.

Hifrance Cottage $$ Scott's
Head ☎ 448-2937. One unit.

Honychurch Apartment $
Roseau ☎ 448-3346.One unit.

Indian River Inn $ Prince Rupert
Bay ☎ 445-5288. Situated on the
beach at the southern end of
Portsmouth, and offering 12 self-
contained apartments.

Itassi Cottages $ Morne Bruce
☎ 448-4313. 3 units. Self catering
well-appointed cottages with
fabulous views of the Caribbean
and a 15 minute walk from
Roseau. Tennis.

Layou Valley Inn Cottages $
Layou Valley ☎ 449-6203. 3 units.
It has a restaurant and pool.

Lydiaville $ Scott's Head
☎ 448-4313. 2 units.

Papillote Wilderness Retreat $$
2 Trafalgar. ☎ 448-2287. Set in the
Papillote Nature Sanctuary with
accommodation among the trees.
The Rainforest Restaurant is open

Facing page: Rosalie River

for lunch every day including Sunday. Reservations for dinner are required.

Petit Coulibri Guest Cottages $
Soufriere ☎ 446-3150. The cottages are scattered in the grounds of the estate which is 1,000ft (305m) above sea level and has fine views south across the waters to Martinique. Self catering facilities are provided but meals are available. There is a large pool.

Picard Beach Cottage Resort $$
Picard ☎ 445-5131. A lovely setting with 8 bungalows on the beach, 1 mile (2km) south of Portsmouth. It has Le Flambeau restaurant, pool, conference facilities and offers honeymoon and diving packages.

Pointe Baptiste $ Calibishie Village ☎ 445-7322. 2 units.

Pringle Self Catering Apartments $ Belfast ☎ 448-2630. 7 units.

Red Rock Haven $ Calibishie ☎ 448-2181. 3 units. Three chalets with maid service by the beach close to Calibishie.

Sango's Sea Lodge $ Picard Beach, Picard Estate, Portsmouth ☎ 445-5211. It has a restaurant.

Sans Souci Manor $$
St. Aroment ☎ 448-2306. 4 units. It has a pool.

White Cottages $ Glasgow ☎ 448-2028. 3 units.

AIRLINES/AIRPORTS

Air Guadeloupe ☎ 448-2181
BWIA International ☎ 809-462-0262 and 1-800-538-2942 in the USA. In the US 1-800-JET-BWIA
Cardinal Airlines ☎ 449-0322
Carib Express ☎ 1 800 744 3333 from the Windward Islands, ☎ 809-431-9200 from other locations
Caribbean Air Services ☎ 449-1748
LIAT ☎ 448-2421
WINAIR ☎ 448-2181

BANKS

Banks are open Monday to Thursday 8am-3pm, and from 8am-5pm on Fridays. Banks are generally closed at weekends and on public holidays.

Agricultural, Industrial and Development Bank
64 Hillsborough Street, Roseau ☎ 448-2853.

Banque Francaise Commerciale
Queen Mary Street, Roseau
☎ 448-4040.

Barclays Bank
Old Street, Roseau ☎ 448-2571,
and in Portsmouth, ☎ 445-5271.

National Commercial Bank of Dominica
64 Hillsborough Street, Roseau
☎ 448-4401, Portsmouth
☎ 445-5430.

Royal Bank of Canada
Bay Front, Roseau ☎ 448-2771.

Scotiabank (Bank of Nova Scotia)
28 Hillsborough Street, Roseau.
☎ 448-5800

CAMPING

There are no camping facilities on the island and sleeping out, especially on the beach, is not allowed.

CAR RENTAL

Cars and 4 wheel drive vehicles can be hired and provide the best way of exploring the island. If you plan to go at peak periods, it is best to hire your vehicle in advance through your travel agent. Cars can be hired, however, at airports, hotels or car hire offices on the island.

Hire car rates start from around US$250 a week depending on the type of vehicle and the rental company. Average daily rates start around US$35 and this does not include insurance which costs an additional US$15-20 a day.

A temporary Dominican driving licence is required, and can be obtained on production of your current driving licence on arrival at the airport on any day of the week, the car hire office, or weekdays from the Traffic Department in the High Street, Roseau. The licence costs EC$20 for 1 month or EC$ 45 for 3 months. Drivers must be aged between 25 and 65, and have at least 2 years driving experience.

Rules of the Road

DRIVE ON THE LEFT. The roads are generally good and there is a substantial road improvement programme under way. In rural areas, however, you have to be on the look out for potholes, fallen branches, coconuts in the roads and so on. Do not speed because you never know what may be round the next corner. The Dominicans love of cricket encourages them to play at every opportunity, and the road makes an ideal wicket!

Seat belts are not compulsory

but is is advisable to wear them at all times. The speed limit is 30mph (48kph) or lower in town, and there is no reason to go very much faster out of town because you will not fully appreciate the scenery.

Drinking and driving is against the law, and there are heavy penalties if convicted, especially if it resulted in an accident.

Avoid clearly marked 'no parking' zones or you might pick up a ticket, but parking generally does not pose a problem.

If you have an accident or breakdown during the day, call your car hire company, so make sure you have the telephone number with you. They will usually send out a mechanic or a replacement vehicle. If you are stuck at night make sure the car is off the road, lock the vehicle and call a taxi to take you back to your hotel. Report the problem to the car hire company or the police as soon as possible.

Hire companies include:
Anslem's Car Rental, 3 Great Marlborough Street, Roseau ☎ 448-2730.
Avis, 4 High Street, Roseau ☎ 448-2481.
Bonus Rentals, Fond Cole, Roseau ☎ 448-2650.
Budget Rent-a-Car, Canefield Industrial Estate, Canefield ☎ 449-2080.

Ken's Taxi Service, 62 Hillsborough Street, Roseau ☎ 448-4850.
S.T.L. Rent-a-Car, Goodwill Road, Roseau ☎ 448-2340.
Sag Rent-a-Car, Canefield ☎ 449-1093.
Valley Rent-a-Car, Goodwill Road, Roseau ☎ 448-32330, and Portsmouth ☎ 445-5252.
Wide Range Car Rentals, Bath Road, Roseau ☎ 448-2198.

CHURCHES

Three quarters of the population are Roman Catholic but most major denominations are represented on the island including Anglican, Methodist, Pentacostal, Baptist, Church of Christ, Seventh Day Adventist, Jehovah's Witness and Baha'i. Many of these denominations hold nightly prayer meetings or services, and visitors are always made welcome. Hotels generally have details about times of church services and locations.
Locations are:
Roman Catholic Cathedral, Virgin Lane, Roseau.
Anglican Church, Victoria Street, Roseau.
Methodist Church, Cross Street, Roseau.
Pentecostal Church, Goodwill.

Berean Bible, 1 Good Road,
    Roseau.
Christian Union, Rose Street,
    Roseau.
Deliverance Baptist, Federation
    Drive, Roseau.
Trinity Baptist, Kings Hill, Roseau.
Seventh Day Adventist, Goodwill
    Road.
Baha'i Faith, Newtown, Roseau.
Qahal Yahweh, 47 Wattey's Lane,
    Goodwill.

CLOTHING

Casual is the keyword but you can
be as smart or as cool as you like.
Beachwear is fine for the beach and
pool areas, but cover up a little for
the street. Informal is the order of
the day and night, and this is not the
place for suits and ties or evening
gowns, unless you really like
dressing up for dinner. During the
day, light cotton, casual clothes are
ideal for exploring in. During the
evening, a light jumper may
sometimes be needed. It is fun to
change for dinner, but for men this
normally means smart slacks or
trousers, and for women a summer
dress or similar. If you plan to
explore inland on foot, stout
footwear and a good waterproof
jacket are essential. Also, wear
sunglasses and a hat to protect you
from the sun during the hottest part

of the day, and on the beach you
will need sandals as the sand can
get too hot to walk. Topless bathing
is not allowed on any of the islands
(except Martinique). It may be
possible, discreetly, at private hotel
beaches, but is still frowned on.

CURRENCY

The official currency on the island is
the East Caribbean dollar although
US dollars are accepted almost
everywhere. EC$ come in the
following denominations: 5, 10, 20,
50 and 100, with 1c, 2c, 5c, 10c,
25c, 50c and one dollar coins.

The banks offer a fixed, and
generally a better rate of exchange
than hotels and shops. Travellers
cheques, preferably in US dollars,
are also accepted in hotels and
large stores, and all major credit
cards can be used in hotels, large
stores and restaurants. The
American Express local
representative is Whitchurch
Travel in Old Street, Roseau
(☎ 448-2181).

Note: Always make certain that
you know what currency you are
dealing in when arranging a taxi
ride, guide, charter and so on.
First establish the currency (either
EC$ or US$) and then agree a
price. It could save a lot of
arguments later on. Always have a

few small denomination notes, either US$1 or EC$5 notes for tips.

DEPARTURE TAX

There is a departure tax of EC$20 (US$8) for all passengers aged 12 or over leaving the island after a stay of more than 24 hours, and a EC$5 (US$2) security charge. The tax can be paid in either EC or US dollars.

DISABLED FACILITIES

There are some facilities for the disabled at most of the larger resorts, but not much elsewhere.

ELECTRICITY

The usual electricity supply is 220/240 volts, 50 cycles, and supplied by Dominica Electricity Supplies, a largely state-owned company. About 70 per cent of the island's power supply comes from hydro-electric schemes, and the remainder is provided by diesel generators.

Some hotels also have 110 volt supplies which are suitable for US appliances. Adaptors, however, are generally available at the hotels, or can be purchased if you do not travel with your own.

EMERGENCY TELEPHONE NUMBERS

For Police, Fire and Ambulance dial 999.

ENTERTAINMENT

Most of the hotels have some evening entertainment but this largely consists of live music over dinner. The Anchorage has a poolside barbecue on Thursday evenings, the Evergreen Hotel has live music and dinner on Friday evenings, and the Fort Young Hotel has live music over dinner on Wednesday and Sunday with live music in the open air bar area on Saturday nights. The Garraway Hotel has live music in the bar on Friday nights. The Lauro Club Hotel has live music featuring traditional island song and dance on Wednesday, and the Reigate Waterfront features live entertainment as part of its Wednesday night barbecue.

There are weekend discos at Aqua Cade in Canefield, and The Warehouse in Checkhall, while other nightime entertainment spots in Roseau include Trends, the Pina Colada Bar, Etienne's Garden Club at Clarke Hall, Good Times at Checkhall, and the Night Box.

ESSENTIAL THINGS TO PACK

Sun tan cream, sunglasses, sun hat, camera (and lots of film), insect repellant, binoculars if interested in bird watching and wildlife, and a small torch in case of power failures.

FERRIES

There are regular scheduled ferries from both Martinique and Guadeloupe to Dominica. These are provided by Caribbean Express, ☎ 448-2181, and Madikera, ☎ 448-6977.

FESTIVALS/PUBLIC HOLIDAYS

January
New Year's Day

February
Carnival

April
Good Friday
Easter Monday

May
May 1st

June
Whit Monday (Pentecost)

June and July
Fishing villages separate the Feast of St. Peter and St. Paul. Villages celebrate on different days so that people can attend them all. During the ceremony, the fishermen, their boats and nets are blessed by the local clergy.

August
August Bank Holiday

November
1st All Saint's Day
3rd Independence Day
4th Community Services Day

December
25th Christmas Day
26th Boxing Day

FISHING

Fishing is an island pursuit, and many Dominicans will fish for hours from harbour walls, from the beach or river side. Deep sea and game fishing is mostly for blue marlin and tuna which can weigh up to 1,000lb (450kg) wahoo and white marlin, which can weigh more than 100lb (45kg) and the fighting sailfish. Snapper, grouper, bonito, dorado and

Rosalie Sugar Mill showing the ruins of the waterwheel (left) and the aqueduct

barracuda can all be kept close to shore. There are a number of boats available for charter or which offer deep sea fishing. Operators include: Gamefishing Dominica, Castle Comfort ☎ 448-2638.

HEALTH

There are no serious health problems although visitors should take precautions against the sun and mosquitoes, both of which can ruin your holiday. Immunisation is not required unless travelling from an infected area within 6 days of arrival. All hotels have doctors either resident or on call.

A Yellow Fever vaccination is required if arriving or in-transit from an infected area.

HOSPITALS

The main hospitals are the Dominica Infirmary on Queen Mary Street, Roseau, and Princess Margaret Hospital, Goodwill, Roseau.

HURRICANES

Dominica is on the hurricane belt and has been hit by three hurricanes in recent years – Hurricane David in 1979, Hurricane Allen in 1980 and Hurricane Hugo in 1989. Hurricane season is between August and early October, with September the most likely month for tropical storms, although thankfully, most of these pass safely well north of the island. Weather stations track all tropical storms and give considerable warning of likely landfall.

IMPORT/EXPORT RESTRICTIONS

Dominica has strict import regulations covering plants, fruit and straw materials in order to protect the island's disease free status as an agricultural producer. There is ban on the import of bananas and coconut fruit, as well as citrus, coffee, avocado fruit and soil. All plants brought in must be accompanied by a phytosanitary certificate and presented for inspection. There is also a ban on the export of produce such as live crabs, crayfish and other forms of wildlife without a permit.

IRRITATING INSECTS

Mosquitoes can be a problem almost anywhere. In your room, burn mosquito coils or use one of the many electrical plug in devices which burn an insect repelling tablet. Mosquitoes are not so much of a problem on or near the beaches because of onshore winds, but they may well bite you as you enjoy an open air evening meal. Use a good insect repellant, particularly if you are planning trips inland such as walking in the rain forests. Lemon grass can be found growing naturally, and a handful of this in your room is also a useful mosquito deterrent.

Sand flies can be a problem on the beach. Despite their tiny size they can give you a nasty bite. Ants abound, so make sure you check the ground carefully before sitting down otherwise you might get bitten, and the bites can itch for days. There are several creams and sprays available to relieve itchiness from bites and Bay Rum Cologne is also a good remedy when dabbed on the skin.

LANGUAGE

The official language spoken is English, although most people speak a French patois.

LOST PROPERTY

Report lost property as soon as possible to your hotel or the nearest police station.

MEDIA

Dominica has four radio stations: DBS (AM 595Khz, FM 88.1MHz), VO1 (AM 860Khz, FM 96.1MHz), VOL (AM 1060Khz, FM 102.9 and 90.6Mhz), and Radio GNBA Mango (FM 93.5Mhz).

There are two pay cable television stations: Marpin TV has nine channels, and Video 1. Nationally broadcast US channels are also usually available.

MUSIC

Music is a way of life and the philosophy is the louder it is played, the better. Cars, mini-van buses and open doorways all seem to blast music out, and once the music starts it goes on for hours. When the Dominicans party, it often lasts all night.

PERSONAL INSURANCE & MEDICAL COVER

Make sure you have adequate personal insurance and medical cover. If you need to call out a doctor or have medical treatment, you will probably have to pay for it at the time, so keep all receipts so that you can reclaim on your insurance.

PHARMACIES

Roseau: City Drug Store, Cork and Old Streets ☎ 448-3198, Dominica Dispensary, 9a Church Street ☎ 448-2938, Jolly's Pharmacy, 37 Great George Street ☎ 448-3388, Kays Pharmacy, 29 Cork Street ☎ 448-2051, New Charles Pharmacy, Angle Fields & Cross Lane, Roseau ☎ 448-3198.

PHOTOGRAPHY

The intensity of the sun can play havoc with your films, especially if photographing near water or white sand. Compensate for the brightness or your photographs will come out over exposed. The heat can actually damage film so store reels in a box or bag in the hotel fridge if there is one. Also remember to protect your camera if on the beach, as a single grain of sand is all it takes to jam your camera.

It is very easy to get 'click happy' in the Caribbean, but be tactful when taking photographs. Many islanders are shy or simply fed up with being photographed, and others will insist on a small payment. You will have to decide whether the picture is worth it, but if a person declines to have their photograph taken, do not ignore this. The islanders are a warm and very hospitable race and if you stop and spend some time finding out what they are doing, they will usually then allow you to take a photograph.

Film developing: Depex Colour Lab, Cork Street, Roseau ☎ 448-2012, and Photoworld, 26 King George V Street, Roseau ☎ 448-4707, both offer a one hour full colour developing service.

POLICE

Police Headquarters is on the corner of King George V Street and Bath Road, Roseau. ☎ 448-2222.

PORTS

The main port is Portsmouth

although there are deep water facilities in Woodbridge Bay just outside Roseau. There are also marinas.

POST OFFICE

The General Post Office is on Bay Street Roseau, and is open 8am-4pm Monday to Friday. There are sub-post offices in Portsmouth and some large villages.

PUBLIC TOILETS

There are not many public toilets on the island, but bars, restaurants and hotels have private facilities which can usually be used if you ask politely.

RESTAURANTS

There is a remarkably large choice when it comes to eating out on the island. There are the inevitable fast food burger, pizza and fried chicken outlets, beach cafés offering excellent value for the money, and elegant upmarket dining rooms, as well as restaurants offering a wide range of ethnic cuisines, from creole and Caribbean cooking to Chinese.

Most accept credit cards and during peak times of the year, reservations are recommended.

Most restaurants are closed on Saturday afternoons and all day Sunday, but hotel restaurants are open daily and welcome outside guests. The restaurants listed in the itineraries are classified by price ($ inexpensive, $$ moderate, $$$ expensive).

SECURITY

Dominica has a low crime rate but it makes sense like anywhere else, not to walk around wearing expensive jewellery or flashing large sums of money.

Do not carry around your passport, travellers cheques or all your money. Keep them secure in your room or in a hotel safety deposit box. It is also a good idea to have photocopies of the information page of your passport, your air ticket and holiday insurance policy. All will help greatly if the originals are lost.

As with most tourist destinations, you might be pestered by touts trying to sell tours, souvenirs and even drugs, or by young people begging. A firm 'no' or 'not interested', is normally enough to persuade them to try someone else. Do not be alarmed at the large numbers of people who walk around with machetes. These are used throughout the island as a gardening implement.

SERVICE CHARGES & TAXES

There is a Government tax of 5 per cent on all hotel rooms, and a Government Sales Tax of 3 per cent. A 10 per cent service charge may also be added to restaurant bills. Menus and tariffs sometimes include these charges so check to make sure they have not been added again. In shops, the price on the label is generally what you pay but when buying in markets and from street vendors, try haggling over the price.

SIGHTSEEING & TOURS

Sightseeing and island tours by land or sea can be organised through hotels, tour representatives or one of the many specialist tour companies on the island.
These include:

Alex Forest Tours ☎ 448-2831.

Anisons Tours, Woodstone Shopping Mall, Cork Street, Roseau ☎ 448-6460.

Antours, Woodstone Shopping Mall, Roseau ☎ 448-6460. Hiking tours with guides, sightseeing tours.

Astaphan Tours ☎ 448-3221.

Didier's Tours, Greens Lane, Goodwill, Roseau ☎ 448-3706. Offers half day and day tours, hikes, birdwatching, photo safaris, scuba diving.

Dominica Tours, Anchorage Hotel, Castle Comfort, Roseau ☎ 448-2638. Offers scuba, diving and water sports, whale watching, island tours and hiking.

Emerald Safaris ☎ 448-4545.

Ken's Hinterland Adventure Tours, Roseau ☎ 448-4850. Day tours and longer for sightseeing, hiking, photo safaris and birdwatching.

Linton's Tours, Elmshall, Roseau ☎ 448-2558.Sightseeing tours by hour, half day and day, hikes with guides.

Mally's Tour & Taxi Service, 64 Cork Street, Roseau ☎ 448-3114. Sightseeing day tours including drinks and lunch and tours by the hour to view sights of interest, plus hikes, bird watching, photo safaris and personalised itineraries.

Mussons Travel, Old Street, Roseau ☎ 448-2550.

Nature Island Tours, Roseau ☎ 448-3397, offering photo safaris and hikes.

Paradise Tours, Steber Street, Pottersville, Roseau ☎ 448-5999. Island tours and tours to specific attractions.

Pierro Nature Safari, King George V Street, Roseau ☎ 448-2292. Offers island tours, trail hiking and photo safaris.

Rainbow River Tours, Roseau ☎ 448-8650. Day trips around the island, week-end packages, overnight hikes.

Sun Link Tours, Dorset House, Roseau ☎ 448-2552. Offers a wide range of sea and land excursions.

Whitchurch Travel Agency, Old Street, Roseau ☎ 448-2181. Offers day tours.

Wilderness Adventure Tours, Bath Road, Roseau ☎ 448-2198. Offers naturalist and photo safari tours, wild and tame garden tours, and hikes.

SPORT

Cricket is the national game and played with such a fervour that it is not surprising that the West Indies are world champions. The game is played at every opportunity and anywhere. You can be driving in the countryside, turn a corner and confront players using the road as a wicket. It is played on the beach and even in the water if the tide is coming in.

If the island team or the West Indies is playing, almost all the radios on the island are tuned in for the commentary. When cricket is not being played, football is the top sport.

For the visitor, there is a huge range of sporting opportunities from swimming and scuba diving, to hiking and tennis. There is cycling, sailing, squash and, of course, fishing either from shore or boat. The Atlantic coastline offers stronger swell for windsurfing and surfing but the seas can sometimes be very rough and care is needed.

Most hotels offer a variety of sports and water activities, and there are diving schools where you can learn what it is all about and progress to advanced level if you have the time.

Walking is great fun and there are lots of trails, especially in the mountains but have stout, non-slip footwear and a waterproof. Protect yourself against insects, carry adequate drinking water and keep an eye on the time, because night falls quickly and you do not want to be caught out on the trail after dark. Guides can be arranged to escort you on these walks and make sure you get the most out of your trip.

Fitness Gyms/Health Centres

Carlian Aerobic and Dance Centre, Old Street, Roseau ☎ 448-6602. Mac's Health Club, Old Street, Roseau ☎ 448-8050.

Hiking

There are some spectacular walks on Dominica ranging from the easy to the long and strenuous. If you are planning to walk to remote interior locations it is advisable to hire a guide for the trip. Guides can be arranged at very reasonable cost, and they will ensure that you get the most out of your trip and find your way back. Dominica offers great walking but the going can be tough not only because of the steepness of some of the terrain, but also because of the heat and humidity. It is essential to drink plenty of water and take frequent rests, as the walking may be more tiring than you realise. Wear sensible, sturdy footwear, like the island's Benjashoe sandals.

Mountain Biking

This is not for the faint hearted, but is now offered by a number of tour operators.

Scuba Diving

The waters off Dominica offer some of the best diving in the world. The waters are warm and clear, the reefs are easily accessible and they teem with marine life. The best diving areas are around the Cabrits National Park and Douglas Bay on the north-west coast, and around Scotts Head on the south-western tip of the island.

Divers should hold a Certified Diver's Card unless signing up with a diving centre to undergo training. Diving should only be carried out with the authority of an authorised diving centre operator, and a permit is required from one of these authorised dive operations on the island or the Fisheries Development Division in Roseau. The catching of fish or other living organism from reefs or seabed is forbidden, as is the removal of any objects from wrecks. The use of spearguns is not allowed.

The following offer diving training, tours and watersports:

Anchorage Dive Centre, Castle Comfort, Picard and Portsmouth ☎ 448-2638.
Dive Castaways, Mero ☎ 449-6244.
Dive Dominica, Castle Comfort ☎ 448-2188.
East Carib Dive, Salisbury ☎ 449-6602.
Nature Island Dive, Soufrière

☎ 449-8181.
Windward Island Divers,
Portsmouth ☎ 445-5104.

Squash

Anchorage Hotel, Castle
Comfort ☎ 448-2638.

Tennis

There are courts at Castaways
Beach Hotel, Mero ☎ 449-6244,
and Reigate Hall Hotel, Roseau ☎
448-4031.

Water Sports

This is available at all resorts and
most large hotels. Sea kayaking
has recently been introduced,
and is offered by Nature Island
Dive and Ken's Hinterland
Adventure Tours ☎ 448-4850.

TELEPHONES & COMMUNICATIONS

In 1987 Dominica became the first
country in the world to launch a
totally digital telecommunications
system. There are public
telephones around the island, and
telephone, telegram, telefax and
data services are provided by
Cable and Wireless (West Indies)
Ltd, along with International Direct
Dialling and USA Direct. Most
public telephones accept coins
and phone cards. Phone cards
can be purchased at many
locations including hotels, shops,
airports, marinas and tourist
offices. The phone cards can also
be used on most of the English-
speaking Windward Islands. Local
and collect calls can be made
from pay phones, and local,
collect and overseas calls can be
made from card phones. The
international dialling code for
Dominica is 809 plus the seven
digit number. From the United
States, it is a long distance call,
dial 1 809 and the seven digit
number. From the United
Kingdom 00 1 809 and then the
number.

USA Direct calls can be made
from hotels by obtaining an
outside line and dialling 1-800-
872-2881 and then following the
instructions. There are special USA
Direct telephones in the Canefield
Airport departure and arrival
lounges, and at the Cable &
Wireless offices in Roseau. For BT
Direct dial 1-800-744-2284. Just
lifting the handset connects you
to AT&T. For credit card calls, dial
1-800-877-8000 and then follow
the recorded instructions.

Faxes can be sent from most
hotels.

TIME

Dominica operates under Atlantic Standard Time Zone which is 4 hours behind Greenwich Mean Time and one hour ahead of Eastern Standard Time in the United States. If it is 12noon in London it is 8am in Dominica, and when it is 12noon in New York, it is 1pm on the island.

While it is important to know the time so that you do not miss your flight, time becomes less important the longer you stay on the island. If you order a taxi it will generally be early or arrive on time, and if you have a business meeting it will start on schedule, for almost everything else be prepared to adopt 'Caribbean time', especially in bars, restaurants and shops. Do not confuse this relaxed attitude with laziness or rudeness, it is just the way things are done on the islands, and the quicker you accept this, the sooner you will start to relax and enjoy yourselves.

TIPPING

Tips are not generally added to bills but it is customary to tip bell hops in hotels, taxi drivers, guides and other people providing a service. Tip taxi drivers around 10-12 per cent and bell hops EC$1-2 for each piece of luggage.

TOURIST OFFICES

There are tourist information centres in Roseau at the Old Market, in Portsmouth near the cruise docks, and at both airports. There is also a tourist information desk in the arrivals terminal at Antigua's international airport for passengers flying on to Dominica.

The tourist office is part of the **National Development Corporation**, PO Box 293, Roseau, Dominica ☎ 448-2351.

Belgium: OECS Embassy, rue des Aquatiques 100, 1040 Brussels ☎ 322-733-4328.

Canada: OECS Mission, Suite 1050, 112 Kent St. Ottawa, Ontario K1P 5P2 ☎ 613-236-8952.

UK: Caribbean Tourism Organisation, Suite 3/15, Vigilant House, 120 Wilton Road. London SW1V 1JZ ☎ 0171-233-8382.

USA: Caribbean Tourism Organisation, 20 East 46 Street, New York, NY 1001-2452. ☎ 212-682-0435.

WATER

Drinking water from the tap is safe although bottled mineral and distilled water is widely available.